Here Comes Humanity Dick

© John Norman 2006
ISBN 1 897 887 60 4

Published by Natula Publications
Natula, 5 St Margarets Avenue, Christchurch BH23 1JD
www.natula.co.uk

British Library Cataloguing-in-Publication Data.
A catalogue record for this book is available from the British Library.

The publishers would like to thank the Bournemouth Echo, Colin Seddon Photography and the Western Telegraph for allowing us to use photographs from their archives. Other illustrations are the authors own.

Printed in Great Britain by Cromwell Press Limited, Trowbridge

Cover illustrations
Front cover: designed by Paul Corfield
Back cover: RSPCA Inspector John Norman photographed on Tuesday 16th August 2005 at 1700 hours after exactly 35 years in the job.

Preface

On the 16th June 1824 William Wilberforce MP and Richard Martin MP had a meeting in The Old Slaughters Coffee House in London. A London vicar, Arthur Broome, had called this meeting and as a result the R.S.P.C.A. was born.

The London slang for the name Richard was Dick and so as the first inspectors were seen on the streets people would say:

"Here comes Humanity Dick."

Acknowledgements

Special thanks must go to:

Natula Publications for their help and guidance with this project.

Paul, my son-in-law, who designed the front cover and provided the author's photo on the back cover.
www.paulcorfield.com

Sara (pronounced Sarah), my daughter, who transcribed my freehand writing into the typed manuscript.

Sandra, my wife, without whose support and encouragement this book would not have been written. I dedicate this book to her.

Sandra without whom there would not have been the last 35 years.

Contents

CHAPTER 1

I know you will pass!

August 17th 1970 was going to be the day - the day that I started as a trainee RSPCA inspector and after a couple of the worst months in my life I was told by the 'powers that be' at the RSPCA Headquarters where I had been doing my training that if I passed the final exams in December I would be posted to Loughborough as the inspector for that branch. Those final exams started on the Monday morning and would last for the next four days. All the subjects that had been chiselled into my sore brain over the past months needed to be remembered. My confidence was not high. I had only a secondary modern education and in my case that was closer to a third than a secondary. If only I had taken more interest in what the teachers at my school had been telling me maybe my confidence would now be a little higher. "He could do better!" "He should have done better!" "John's work was very good over the year but his exam results are not as good as I would have liked." I remember those words that were written continually on my school reports.

I had a wife and young baby waiting for me at home in Mansfield with tea chests packed in preparation for moving, dependent upon these results. Sandra, my wife, had written in a letter that week saying, "I know you will pass." After I read her letter I thought, if only the person who had told her that would tell those stiff-necked instructors at HQ and me. Monday, Tuesday, Wednesday, Thursday…how the hell did I get to Thursday? My head was going round and round with facts about 'Protection of Animals Act 1911, section 1, subsection 1a', 'Transport of Poultry Act 1919. How much anaesthetic do you give to an animal weighing ten pounds? Was it 1ml for every 3 pounds or 3mls for every 1 pound of body weight? I could not remember. I could the night before as I burned the midnight oil staring into the legal and medical books, but here, sat in a classroom in complete silence trying to get the answer to look good on the exam paper was my greatest nightmare.

Friday morning and some of the early results were being put up on the notice board. The more confident students went to have a look; some just stood staring at the list of results not saying anything. Others moved from side to side as if trying to get a better view but I think it was to keep the blood flowing in their legs. The rest like me, and I think there was only me, sat in the chair at the desk trying to make everyone think that I was being courteous by letting them get closer to the board. The truth was the further away from that board I was the better I felt. "You have not done too bad John," said one of the lads, "not good, but not bad!" I could have killed him. He had no idea what my 'not bad' was, remember those school reports? I walked towards the notice board, well I think I walked but I didn't feel my feet touching the floor. I could not remember whether it was left foot forward then the right, or right foot forward then the left, anyway I must have been on autopilot because I found myself standing about six feet in front of the board.

I could see the list of names, the titles of the subjects and the percent marks that were needed to pass that subject, and the percent marks at the side of each student's name. My head was in such a state that at one point I had forgotten my name. I could see and read everyone else's marks but could not for the life of me see my own name. Had I done that 'not bad' that the examiners had failed to find one single percent that they could give me? Subject 'Humane Destruction' Norman J – 68%, Subject 'Veterinary' 70%, Subject 'Parliamentary Department' 68%, 'Branch Duties' 96%. My eyes had not blinked since they first captured my name on the list. As I followed the line across the paper to the marks I checked that I had not wandered off the right line and was in fact reading someone else's results. Again I checked it and somebody said, "John Norman 96%, you've got to be joking! What did you take into the exam room with you John, all the bloody questions?" "No," I said with all the confidence of my wife, "all the bloody answers." Everybody laughed and started to shake hands as we read each other's results. All of us had passed the final exams.

CHAPTER 2

January 8th 1971

Friday, January 8th 1971 and we (that's me and my new colleagues as I now called the lads that had been my mates for the last few months) collected our Bedford vans from the Society's Transport Department at Chobham. Some of the vans were grey in colour, some deep blue. I got a deep blue one. "Good," I thought. Everyone wanted to have a deep blue van as these looked like the vans used by the police and with our dark uniforms motorists thought they had a police vehicle behind them and more often than not they gave way and allowed us to pass. I drove from Chobham up towards the M1. In front of me was Chris, who had been posted to Nuneaton, Brian who was on his way to some far outpost up north, and then me, followed by two others who would use the M1 to take them home and then onwards to their new stations and their new homes for the next seven years. As I drove up the M1 towards Mansfield, my home address, I was excitedly thinking about my new station. I had been posted to Loughborough. During our six months training we were sent out into the field with a chief inspector. One of my field training duties had been with Chief Inspector Harfleet, who lived in Leicester. Jim Harfleet was a gentleman in every sense of the word. I worked for one month with Jim and one day we visited the Society's house in Loughborough. There was no inspector working in this area and I was given a strong hint from Jim that if all went well with my final exams I could find myself living in this very house.

Well here I was driving up the M1 to Mansfield where Sandra had organised the furniture removal van to collect our things first thing the following morning. She told me that Peter my young son, who was too young to know what was going on, had found the art of unpacking as quickly as Sandra had packed and as fast as she put things away he took them out again. Anyway all was ready and waiting for Saturday morning. The removal van arrived punctually and in no time at all our bits and bobs were safely on board, not that there was a lot to take on board. We had been married for two years and our '2 up - 2 down' did not hold a lot. We had only been in the house for twenty-three months. The house cost £999. Yes it did, £999, and that was a down payment of £100 and a £25 a month mortgage. We had the house on the market but we could not go through with the sale until I knew I had passed the exams. It had not been on the market long so the mortgage people had agreed to take back the house as it stood and with the money we had spent on it and the mortgage payments we had already paid would call it square. Having left the keys with the estate agents in Mansfield we made our way to our new home in Loughborough.

Sandra had not seen the new house. I had told her what I could remember about it, but on arrival it all seemed so different from what I had envisaged seeing a few months before. It seemed strange. I knew that people could leave one way of life, their home town, family and friends and move lock, stock and barrel to an unknown place (where sometimes you had to look on a map to find out where it was) but that's how it was. There was no going to view a house or looking around the area to see if you liked the place. Inspectors in the Society signed a deed of contract stating that they could be stationed anywhere in England or Wales and that they would live in the property owned by the Society. They could also expect to be moved every seven years.

Well, here we were! Sandra had explored all the rooms and given it the thumbs up. There had been a third bedroom added to the house and building this had given us an enormous kitchen area underneath this bedroom. The sound of our voices in the kitchen echoed and Peter could ride his bike up and down as he had a clear run from one end of the kitchen to the other. Little did we know that we were only going to spend some eighteen months in this house. My time in Loughborough's branch was good and I enjoyed everyday. I remember those first few days in uniform. As I walked past a shop window I could not resist having a look at my reflection. We had big gold coloured stars on our epaulettes. They were very big and we used to call them 'dustbin lids' but I was very proud of my uniform. Now some people look good in a uniform. Others, no matter what they do, do not seem to do it any justice. But I was lucky; I looked the part when I left the house in the mornings. I was an inspector in the Royal Society for the Prevention of Cruelty to Animals. I represented the Society and was proud to be doing the job.

The first few days were spent meeting various branch officials. These were the locals who had formed a branch for the Society and organised fundraising events so that they could help the animals in their branch. I was employed by the RSPCA Headquarters in London, but my duties required me to assist as much as possible with branch affairs. This I did with great gusto and youthful energy, remember my 'Branch Duties' marks? My main duty was to prevent, where possible, suffering to animals. That meant investigating complaints made by the members of the public when they had seen or heard something that they felt was cruel. This could range from neighbours' cats, dogs, birds in aviaries, animals seen on farms, animals that were being offered for sale in pet shops and other such places. The general public are in fact the eyes and ears of the Society. You do not have to be a member of the Society to get action. Anybody could contact me and report whatever it was they felt was wrong.

It was my job to carry out an investigation into those calls, using my new-found knowledge of the law and the Society's policies on animal welfare, and take whatever action I deemed necessary to alleviate any suffering or neglect to the animals, whether that neglect was wilful or through ignorance. I also had to visit establishments that kept or displayed animals such as zoos, circuses, riding stables, slaughterhouses, and knackers' yards; possibly the most important were the cattle markets. In my area I had three cattle markets to see to: one at Market Harborough, one in Loughborough and one of the largest in the country at Melton Mowbray. I remember my first day's duty at this market well. In fact it was my second day as an inspector. It was Tuesday the 12th January 1971. I parked my vehicle where it was not visible from the market and literally tried to sneak in without being

5

seen. Taking into account that I was in full uniform and the peak of my brand new hat seemed to be two feet in front of my forehead and those damned 'dustbin lids' on my shoulder were so big that I kept thinking someone was following me every time I caught sight of them out of the corner of my eye, it was an impossible task.

I walked round the outside of the market for a while hoping no one would recognise me and come and ask me a question that I had no idea of the answer to. Gradually, and believe me it was gradually, I got closer to the pens that held the various cattle, pigs and sheep. I stared at each animal held within as if I knew exactly what I was looking at. I was feeling good as a few members of the public had passed me and we exchanged greetings, "Good morning, nice day!" and one woman showing her two young children the cattle said to them as she pointed to me, "That's the man who looks after these poor animals and makes sure those nasty men don't hit the cows with the sticks." She then smiled at me and as she walked past she put her hand on one of my 'dustbin lids' and said, "I don't know what we would do without you here!" I smiled back at her and carried on with my duties. Now I have never been a tall bloke, only 5ft 7in on my tiptoes, but after what this lady had just said I found myself stooping to get my body through the 6ft 6in doorways. I was still on cloud nine when it happened! I walked right into the farmers waiting for the sale to start. There must have been every farmer in Leicestershire and Nottinghamshire there. Well, at least it looked like there was. Remember my leg movements as I went to the notice board to check my exam results? Well, they were back!

The sound of all these voices talking at once now died to an almost cemetery hush till one man standing with a large group of men near the selling arena said, "Now 'ere's the man who can tell us what it is. Come 'ere mate and 'ave a look at this." The men with him stood to one side revealing the inside of the sale ring and there stood the biggest cow I had ever seen. It was whitish in colour, in fact very similar to my skin at that moment in time. It had a huge lump at the base of its neck that sort of flopped over to one side.

I had seen this animal before on the television, in pictures and in books. Now I knew it wasn't a Jersey cow, or a Guernsey or a Friesian. Why couldn't it have been one of them? No it had to be this enormous, unrecognisable beast - yet if I had seen it on television that night I would have said to Sandra straight away what it was. But it wasn't on the television. It was standing right in front of me at Melton Mowbray Cattle Market on my second day as an RSPCA inspector.

The enormous beast with no name.

I looked at the beast and beast looked at me and I looked at the farmer, the one with the problem of not knowing what sort of beast it was, or so he said. Now I've always had this canny knack of thinking on my feet, you know to get out of trouble, you just ask my mam! Anyway I said to this farmer, "I will tell you what it's not." He said, "What do you mean what it's not?" I said, "It's not suffering." There was complete silence then a titter, then a loud laugh and within seconds everyone was laughing and pointing to the problem farmer. "You see," I said, "as long as it's in good health and not being caused unnecessary suffering then I'm not really bothered if it's a Jersey cow or a Guernsey cow," and then like a flash in the dark it came to me what it was, "or even," I said pointing to the large beast, "this Brahma Bull." I received more pats on my 'dustbin lids' and I made my exit stooping a little lower this time to get out of the 6ft 6in doorway.

Later that day I ventured inside the tearoom for a coffee and who should be propping up the bar but the problem farmer. He saw me in the doorway, I had now receded to my natural height, and he waved me over and said, "Drink on me, Inspector, you'll do for me!" I was only in Loughborough for eighteen months and those lads at the market, including 'Henry' the problem farmer, became great people to work with. Yes work with; it was not my job to go around criticizing and persecuting every move owners and people responsible for animals made, but to aid and assist, to help and advise, to protect and put the 'P' in the Society's name into action. If I had to give words of advice to a drover handling the animals, as they were loading or unloading animals, I tried to talk to them, as I would have wanted them to talk to me if our roles in life were reversed. There were times however, I'm sorry to say, when talking and advice were too late. This was the case on Tuesday 13th April 1971 when I investigated a report that a dog had been found alive in a wire snare and that other spring traps had been set illegally in a local wood. This was the first of many investigations that would end up in the local Magistrates' Court.

CHAPTER 3

That first cruelty case in court

During the first few months in 1971 a national postal strike was taking place and the mail from our London HQ was being dispatched to various chief inspectors, and then relayed around the country to the inspectorate staff. I collected my mail each week from Chief Inspector Harfleet in Leicester along with the mail for the Nottinghamshire and Derbyshire inspectors. I travelled to Mansfield and passed this onto the inspectors. As Mansfield was my hometown I was able to use this trip to visit my mam and dad and Sandra's mam and dad.

The first months had been fairly quiet, as I had been settling into my new job and my new way of life. I had investigated a number of complaints of cruelty to various animals and had given advice to the owners on providing better welfare conditions. In April I had a report from a man who lived in a small village in my branch area. He told me that a few days previously he had lost his Labrador dog whilst walking near some woods. He had been searching for several days but failed to find the dog. He said that his dog knew the area very well and the man couldn't understand why the dog had not found its way home, or that no one in the village had seen his dog. He did go on to say that the reason he contacted me was to tell me that his dog had returned home after being missing for four days. He had noticed that there was a large wound around the dog's waist, very close to the hip area. The man had taken the dog to his own vet and on examining the dog the vet had stated that he thought the dog had been caught in a wire snare. The vet had treated the wound and told this man to inform the RSPCA.

Being given this information I made a visit to the man's home and saw the dog for myself. I could see that the wound around the waist was still sore. It was fairly deep but had not needed to be stitched by the vet. The wound faded out around the body of the dog into a graze, and the dog and its injuries were responding to the veterinary treatment. I went to see the vet who had treated the dog and he confirmed that in his opinion the dog could have been in a wire snare, that the injuries were consistent with this possibility and that the wound was also consistent with the dog being caught in the snare for several days. This information was enough for me to make a full investigation.

It is lawful to set a wire snare on private land as long as it is not near any public right of way where any domestic animal could reasonably be expected to be and the person who sets the snare checks that snare between sunrise and sunset each day. Now with the vet saying that in his opinion the wound on the dog was a day or so old, it was possible that I had someone in the area setting wire snares and not checking them within the time set out by law.

I interviewed several people in the village and took statements from them. One or two told me that they had been in the woods where the dog went missing and had seen wire snares set. I found that these woods were on private land and were owned by one of the local dignitaries. He was farming the land around the woods and was allowing the woods to be worked by one of his employees in the act of game keeping. I found out where this employee lived and went to his home on two separate occasions. I was told that he wasn't in and as he worked unsocial hours I couldn't be advised on the best time to see him. Owing to the type of work he was doing as a gamekeeper it was very hard for anyone to tell me exactly where he might be at any one time.

Having been given this nonsense I took the bull by the horns, so to speak, and went to visit the landowner. He in turn saw me off his land pretty quickly by indicating in strong language that the RSPCA should have better things to do, and in any case his man would have nothing to do with snares not being checked, especially if one had a dog caught in it. The gent then took great pleasure in telling me that there were signs around his woods stating that the woods were 'Private', and to 'Keep out' and that 'Trespassers would be prosecuted'. I was equally pleased to inform him that to date I had not heard that dogs could read, or indeed had the intelligence to know what was, or was not private land. I left the premises of this gentleman farmer feeling that we had both scored points but felt that my manner towards him, and my attitude had not helped me. I'm sure I could hear my bosses in the RSPCA HQ saying that I could have, and should have handled it differently. But when you are out there where the bullets are real and the punches hurt you are on your own and you have to stand your ground. I was very proud to be wearing my RSPCA uniform and I was equally proud of what the RSPCA stood for and no one was going to convince me that the investigation I was carrying out wasn't necessary.

The type of snare that the dog was more than likely caught in was a free running snare. This is simply a wire noose that is attached to an anchor point to prevent the caught animal escaping. The animal is usually caught by its neck but many animals are snared by the leg or around the waist and the more it struggles the tighter the wire snare becomes and the greater the animal suffers. Snares are set for foxes or rabbits but the snare doesn't discriminate between the different animals. If a dog or cat gets caught then the snare carries out its painful hold on its victim. There is a self-locking snare that operates by a ratchet-like mechanism. This means every time the poor animal moves the snare tightens that little bit more and locks into place. Can you begin to imagine the pain and suffering that this causes the animal? The RSPCA were pressing Parliament to change the law making it an offence to use these types of traps, but as things stood in 1971 both snares were unfortunately legal if the setter put them in the right place and inspected them at least once a day. I had seen photographs at HQ during my training that showed animals caught in snares. Unfortunately some of these animals had received horrendous injuries. Some of the photographs showed foxes and badgers that had been caught by their legs and these poor animals had gnawed off their own limbs in an attempt to escape. This is upsetting, I know, and this is why I felt the RSPCA did not have, at this moment in time, "anything better to do than investigate a dog caught in a snare."

One good thing that did come out of my visit to the landowner was that, after he had stated that there was no way there would there be anything out of order in his woods, I asked if he would permit me to inspect the woods so I could assure the local people that this had not been the place where the dog had been caught. I was reluctantly given that permission, so I thought the sooner I inspected the woods the better before the word got out to the gamekeeper or poachers to remove any evidence, that's if it hadn't already been removed.

I found my way into the woods by the nearest route from where the dog went missing. It was a very dense place but the area was kept as a coppice and it had been very well managed. I saw plenty of rabbit holes and runs used by the rabbits. I also saw areas where badgers had been coming and going from a high bank on a sandy ledge but I didn't see any snares. What I did see took me totally by surprise. I could see by standing at the side of a tree just a few feet in front of me an old piece of 4x4 timber. I could not for the life of me think why a piece of wood like this had been brought into the woods. I could see it was about 5 or 6 feet in length and on top it looked as though there was a crude flat-topped bird table. On closer inspection I found that it was in fact an old wooden seed tray that had been nailed to the top of a post. The inside of the tray had been lined with moss to form a sort of nest and on top of this moss there were two pheasant eggs.

I was just about to remove the eggs when I noticed a metal chain coming from underneath the moss and this chain had been nailed to the tree. I took a piece of stick and gently lifted up the moss and I could see that under the moss that the two eggs had been sitting on there was a metal trap. I recognised this as a fen trap. It is a legal trap used for killing or the taking of small ground vermin such as grey squirrels, stoats, weasels, rats and mice. It should be set in a natural or artificial tunnel. Now the perpetrator's reason for setting this trap on top of a pole and hidden under the moss was two fold. When a magpie, crow or other carrion bird that steals eggs, especially pheasant and partridge eggs, comes across this homemade harmless-looking nest and

Owl caught in a Pole Trap
Picture courtesy of Colin Seddon Photography
www.colinseddonphotography.com

peck at the eggs it would set off the trap underneath the moss and trap the bird by whatever part of its body or wing it came into contact with as the trap snapped its jaws closed at lightning speed. If the bird was lucky it would be caught by its head and probably would be killed instantaneously as the jaws of the trap crushed its head, but more times than not the bird would sense the trap and make enough movement to avoid being caught by its head. Instead it would be caught by its leg or wing and now the second part of the perpetrator's plan to set the trap on the pole came into play. The bird caught by its leg or wing would dislodge the trap off the nest and as the trap was securely attached to the tree the bird would hang upside down and die in sheer agony. This type of fixing of a trap was known as a pole trap and it was totally illegal.

So there I was in a private wood, owned by a person who stated nothing illegal was taking place as far as he knew. I had a gamekeeper, somewhere, who was responsible for the woods but as yet we had not spoken. Though by now he had probably spoken to the owner and been informed of my interests. I had a dog that may have been in a wire snare that had not been inspected within the legal times required by law and I had a legal trap that was being used in an illegal manner as it was not being used to catch what it was legally intended for but was being used as an illegal pole trap instead. I was also not happy about the two pheasant eggs. For some reason they just did not fit the bill. Why waste two good eggs? Dummy eggs could have been used over and over again. Anyway I sprung the trap and left it under the moss then I took the eggs and left the woods.

Later that night I contacted my brother-in-law Geoff. Now Geoff was in the Nottinghamshire CID. I asked him if he could get the eggs tested for any poisons that could have been injected into them as I had heard from other more experienced inspectors that eggs are sometimes injected with substances like arsenic by way of a hypodermic needle. Arsenic and other such poisons can be lawfully purchased and used by gamekeepers or any other legitimate exterminator of vermin. Geoff agreed to arrange for the eggs to be examined. I drove over to Southwell where Geoff lived with my sister Janet and left the eggs knowing Geoff would report back to me just as soon as he had any news.

I was up early the next morning, in fact it was about 6.30a.m., and I sat in my vehicle just a few yards up the road from where the elusive gamekeeper lived. As he came out of his house I got out of my vehicle and approached him as he got to his garden gate. Needless to say he was most surprised to see me there at that time in the morning. He confirmed who he was and said that he had heard that I wanted to speak to him. I explained my reasons for this and he agreed that I could go with him on his rounds as he was about to check his traps, pointing out to me that he only used wire snares for rabbits. In the woods we inspected several free running snares that had been properly set at the entrance to rabbit runs. He had been successful on a few occasions in getting his prey. I could see that the rabbits' end had been a swift one, well as swift as a wire snare would allow, and the suffering that had been caused was within the limits permitted by the law.

At this point let me just state a few facts about what our good old English law says about suffering and the causing of that suffering to animals. If I were to say to you, "Is it an offence in this country to cause an animal suffering?" What would be your answer? I expect like most people you would say, "Of course it is an offence!" but I'm sorry you are wrong. You see the law as in the Protection of Animals Act 1911 states that it's only an offence if unnecessary suffering is caused. Pain, no matter how slight, is some form of suffering to an animal, so if a vet injects an animal for whatever reason then he is in fact inflicting some pain. When a vet examines an injured animal to ascertain the extent of that injury and so that they can diagnose the right treatment they may put the animal in some pain. The pain caused is necessary, so you can now see the relevance of the legal wording. If a legal wire snare is 'set properly and is inspected within the laws of setting and inspecting such traps and it is set to catch the intended prey of that trap and the prey is killed legally' any reasonable suffering caused was legal because it was necessary to cause that suffering in order to kill the animal. On the other hand, anyone found to have caused pain to an animal where it can be proved that that pain was unnecessary would be committing an offence, but remember the operative word is 'unnecessary', and that has to be proved in a court of law.

As we walked through the woods I could see that we were getting close to the fen trap I had seen the previous day and I was wondering if it was still there. I noticed that the gamekeeper kept edging away from that area and I, not wanting to give anything away, kept us as close to it as possible until we went right past it but he never made any indication that he had seen it. I felt this was odd as I believed that these gamekeepers knew every stick and tree on their patch and would notice anything unusual or out of place and yet here was such a person walking past a piece of 4x4 timber with a seed tray perched on top of it and he hadn't even noticed it. He must have thought that I had fallen off a Christmas tree. I stood by the timber and said, "What do you reckon this is for then?" He came over to me and looked at the device, took a stick and used this to lift up the moss and expose the fen trap. "I don't know what all this is about," he said, "I've never seen this before." I asked him if anyone else had legal rights to set any traps in the wood and he stated that only he was employed to set traps to keep the vermin down to a manageable level. He did not say anything about the eggs, but if he was denying any knowledge of the trap I did not expect him to mention them and so I said nothing. What I did ask him was why did he not just lift up the moss with his fingers, as I had silently wished he had done, but he just shrugged his shoulders and made no comment.

I removed the 4x4, the seed tray and the fen trap, as he had no objections to me taking them away since they did not belong to him. He told me that he did use fen traps in the wood and he took me to where he had legally and properly set them. I had earlier given him the required caution and informed him of my interest in the dog that had

16

possibly been in a wire snare for several days and that the snare could have been set in this wood. He denied all knowledge of any dog being in the wood or of it being in a wire snare, firmly stating that he inspected his traps twice a day. At the end of the tour I told him that the facts of finding the illegal setting of the fen trap and the injured dog would be reported to my legal department with a view to a prosecution. I again cautioned him and invited him to make a statement or any comment but he declined saying that he would have to have a word with his employer before saying anything else. Later that day Geoff contacted me and said that the tests carried out on the eggs had all been negative.

I made out a case report for my legal department and a few weeks later I was sent the information to lay two summonses against the gamekeeper:

That he did unlawfully set in a position a spring trap being an article of such a nature so placed as to be calculated to cause bodily injury to any wild birds coming into contact therewith, contrary to the Protection of Birds Act 1954, Section 5, Subsection 1a.

That he did unlawfully use an approved trap, namely a fen vermin trap, in circumstances and for a purpose other than that for which it is approved, contrary to Section 81a of the Pest Act 1954 and the Spring Traps Approval Order 1957 as amended.

I was unable to lay information against the gamekeeper for causing unnecessary suffering to the dog, as I could not prove that he had set the snare, or had any knowledge of the dog being caught in the snare. I served the above summonses personally on the gamekeeper and the hearing of the case was set for later in the year.

CHAPTER 4

Operation Swan Watch

Now one of the nicer sides of my job is working with kids. When I went for my interview for the inspectorate I was asked what I thought the biggest aspect of the RSPCA was. Well my answer was then and still is 'Education'. On giving this answer I was asked to explain why I thought it was education. "Well," I said, "what's the point in trying to stop cruelty to animals if the people who we are prosecuting have never been educated about the laws and what's required of them." I felt we must get into the schools and make animal welfare part of the schools' curriculum. The RSPCA does have an education department that does this but I felt we should go into it in more depth and at a higher level.

Anyway a schoolteacher in one of the small villages contacted me and told me that every year around April a pair of swans that lived on the village pond make a nest but as soon as any eggs were laid some idiot disturbs the swans and the eggs always got smashed. The teacher said that this particular year the swans had just started to make a nest right at the side of the fence that ran alongside the road, next to the local junior school. The teacher's concerns were that yet again the swans would not be able to raise any cygnets especially with the nest being so close to the public road. I went to the village and met the teacher who showed me where the swans' nest was. I could see that the swans had been house building for a few days. In fact by the way that they were piling the nesting material onto their site they were going for a 'two up two down' terraced house. The site was indeed up against a small wooden fence that separated the nest from the public pavement. The teacher gave me a history lesson on some of the local kids. Like most kids there were the good, the bad and the ugly but the teacher could not say under which banner the vandals of the swans' eggs came but by using my powers of deduction I eliminated the good and left the latter two.

I went to the junior school and met the head teacher and explained my proposed plan of action. What I wanted was to have a talk with all the pupils at assembly. My idea was not to accuse anyone of vandalism but to educate them on that miraculous feeling of achievement you get when you are able to help and assist wildlife in its struggle with nature, especially when it has to try and adapt to its habitat being invaded by those wonderful humans who had put a footpath alongside the very area they wished to build their own home. At the assembly I explained to the kids that with their parents' permission I was going to ask for volunteers for 'Operation Swan Watch'. I hastened to point out that this would not involve an armed patrol guard as I could see that one or two of the kids that possibly came under the banner of the bad and the ugly seemed to be getting excited. I also told them that this operation would involve the whole village.

The Swans' Nest

I soon had the support of all the people in the village; the local vicar gave the idea a mention in his Sunday service and the local newspaper ran a story with a picture of me and some of the kids. With the help of parents we set up a regular patrol where the swans had started to build their nest, which by now resembled a hotel. They seemed to sense that this year was going to be a good year and they had collected every bit of nesting material that the area could offer. Within a few weeks four eggs were laid and the whole village started to get excited. The big day came and we were rewarded with four lovely cygnets, all four grew and flourished under the watch of our now military-style patrol. The local newspaper and local radio station carried the happy event. I felt sure that from here on in this lovely English village its children would now enjoy seeing cygnets every year.

I was later told by one of the parents that if a visitor came to the village and was seen walking near to the swans' nest, the patrolling children could be heard to say, "Sorry but you cannot walk past the swans, Inspector Norman says so." Do you know what, it doesn't half make you feel good.

CHAPTER 5

You never know what the day will bring

I was beginning to settle very well into the pattern of my new way of life style; each day never ended the way I planned that morning. You could have a dozen or so calls to make where members of the public had requested that you should visit to check on an animal's welfare as they felt it was not being cared for properly. Most of the time the public's definition of an animal not being cared for did not correspond with what the law of the land required the owners to provide. Most of the time I agreed with the callers and pointed out to the owners of the animals that the RSPCA did not agree with the way their animal was being kept or treated but if the law was not being broken my only option was to emphasize to the owners or persons responsible for the welfare of that animal that a better quality of life could be given if they were to carry out a few changes to the animal's daily care. After giving this advice I would, when at all possible, return at a later date to see if my advice was, or had been taken. I am pleased to say that due to the RSPCA's outstanding reputation over many years, combined with our professional training in dealing with both animals and people many of my calls were successful and I saw many animals' lives improve as a result of my visit and that all important first call made by a concerned member of the public.

As I was saying, you never know what the day will bring. There I was driving out of Loughborough one day when I saw in my rear view mirror the flashing blue light of a police patrol car. I slowed down thinking it needed to overtake but the headlights flashed and the passenger police officer was indicating for me to stop. "Now what?" I thought. It can't be drink driving, as I have never had a pint in my life. True that, I never got around to having that first pint. Anyway the police officers got out of their car and came over to me smiling. Now I was worried! "Sorry to stop you, Inspector, we have just called at your house and your missus said you had just left on your way to Melton

Mowbray so we dashed out here and here you are." "Here I am, what's the problem?" Thinking to myself: wife, son, mam, dad other members of the family who could have had an accident. "We have been asked to escort you to Leicester, there's a big circus on there and a vet has asked if you were anywhere in the area could you give him a hand with an elephant?" "An elephant?" I said. "Yeah, a great big thing it is," replied the knowledgeable officer. "Yes I know what an elephant looks like," I said. I also knew what a Brahma bull looked like but I didn't want to confuse the officer. "What's up with the elephant?" I asked. "Don't know really, something about a tent peg," he replied. "Well if a vet is asking for my assistance it must be serious, what vet is it by the way?"

"Don't know that either," said my knowledgeable English bobby. "You follow me." He started to tell me which way we would be going from here into Leicester city centre. Now as the crow flies that was only about five miles but the way my escort was talking, "We will go through so and so village, take a left over such and such a bridge, then go down by so and so's building and then over onto the main road into the city. Take us five minutes tops, just keep up with us and you'll be alright."

Off we went through so and so village, took a left over such and such a bridge, then went down by so and so's building, then over onto the main road and here I was talking to the local vet, whom I did know. He had helped me with a prosecution case a few months before. The vet told me that he had tried to contact other vets in the area but none could be located, then he had been informed that I had been found near Melton and had agreed to attend, of which he was very grateful. He then went on to explain the problem. "You see," he said, "this morning one of the elephants was being taken for a short exercise walk around the site when it stepped on a wooden tent peg. The wedge shaped peg had gone right in between the elephant's toes with the thin edge of the wedge facing up, therefore it was well and truly wedged." We went over to an area behind the main tent and I saw several hired hands gathered around a large, and I mean large, elephant. Two large trucks had been strategically placed each side of the elephant, and two more vehicles were being positioned at the front and rear, thus creating a sort of enclosure with me and all and sundry, including one large unhappy elephant, inside. My first thought was what I intended doing that day. For the life of me I couldn't remember anything in my plans about an elephant and a tent peg.

The handler got the elephant to put its foot up onto one of those large round metal table things that they use when they are performing in the ring and was telling her what a good girl she was. I looked up at the elephant and saw those wonderful round kind eyes that were curtained by the most gorgeous eyelashes that would have made any female movie star jealous. The elephant's trunk was examining the vet, and then it turned its attention on me. It's as though the trunk was frisking us for any sharp instruments but I can assure you that I would not keep any sharp instruments in the places her trunk was going to. The vet told me that he intended to take a carpenter's chisel and try and split the wedge. This would, he hoped, make the wedge loose enough to be removed. He also went on to say that he was unable to administer any sedating drugs. The handler informed us that the elephant was a good girl, well behaved and would not give us any trouble as long as we remained calm whilst carrying out the operation. Sound advice I thought, as yet again her trunk investigated the contents of my crotch.

We managed to remove three good-sized shreds of wood from the wedge, and I used a pair of pliers to remove the remaining offensive piece from the elephant's foot. She in turn examined her foot with her trunk and on her finding that only a covering of antiseptic cream was needed for the sore area, she promptly put her trunk over the vet's shoulder, under his jacket and emptied the contents of his inside pocket out onto the ground. The circus owners had informed the local newspapers of the elephant's predicament and we all starred in the evening editions.

Now later that same day I had arranged to attend one of the local schools where the children had set up a nature table in their classroom.

They had various items of interest displayed such as an old blackbird's nest that showed very clearly how it had been ingeniously woven together by the bird. They had an aquarium tank half filled with soil and several garden worms could be seen making their way underground leaving behind on the surface the soil casts. Leaves had been placed on the surface and you could see how the worms were breaking these down. A second tank contained some ants all busy tunnelling in a sandy soil giving the kids a good view on how the ants organised themselves into a military-style force with every member having its part to play. What a smashing way to teach these kids on how to get on with their neighbours, showing them that in the wild, animals and insects have to show a mutual respect for each other and that everybody has to get on with each other in order to get the various tasks done to enable them to survive.

Anyway, so much for my philosophy on life. My reason for the visit was to hand over some of the RSPCA leaflets on wildlife subjects and to have a general chat about wildlife in the garden. The teacher asked the kids to show me 'Tommy' the classes' pet mouse. This darling little mouse was kept in a large area with lots of different compartments for it to explore. "You can hold Tommy if you like," said one of the kiddies. So I thought why not, I could show off my handling skills to the junior set. I did all the right things, I know I did, but there was something about the index finger on my left hand that dear little Tommy did not like. It sank its teeth into it right to the bone. Now I ask you to tell me what would you do when you are in front of a classroom full of charming little children and the index finger on your left hand had just gone past the paralysed stage, and their little Tommy is hanging on for dear life? Well you smile, of course, and you say things like, "Good boy Tommy, let go of the inspector's finger. You don't want to hurt your teeth now do you?" Those were the words that came out of my mouth, but somewhere deep in my larynx different words were forming and were definitely not for the innocent ears of my young audience.

Eventually Tommy had enough of my finger and he let go. I think it was that nasty blood in his mouth that put him off. Anyway I carefully placed him back in his pen, notice how I used the word 'placed', and on returning him to his home I reminded the children how careful and gentle you have to be when handling pets like Tommy, as it was so very easy to hurt them. I'm sure I heard that teacher laughing, but she assured me she was not and that it was something in her throat that was giving her trouble.

When I look back on that day, which was Thursday, 6th May 1971, I repeat what I always say, "You never know what the day will bring!"

CHAPTER 6

My knowledge of birds

Many RSPCA inspectors come into the Society with their own pet subjects or speciality. Mine was birds, the feathered variety. As a young lad I was always around birds of some sort. My dad was a keeper of racing pigeons and for many of my early years I had helped him at his loft. I learnt that handling the birds was very important if you didn't want to damage the bird's delicate feathers and racing pigeons must be handled as often as possible since what you are doing is building up a trust between the handler and the bird. This is especially important on a race day because when your pigeon arrives back at the loft after flying from its liberation point it has to be caught and a numbered rubber ring has to be removed. This ring would have been placed on the pigeon's leg at the time it was registered in the race. The ring, once removed, is then placed inside a small tumbler, which in turn is placed inside a sealed clock. There is a handle on the clock which when pulled will mark a paper disc inside the clock. When this disc is removed by the official personnel it will tell them at what time each pigeon was 'clocked', down to the last second. The pigeon with the shortest time clocked is the winner. "Easy," I hear you say but "Try it," I say. If you haven't put in the time with handling the birds you will loose valuable seconds trying to catch the pigeon and those lost seconds could cost you the race and possibly thousands of pounds in prize money.

Anyway apart from the pigeons my dad had a great knowledge of wild birds. He could find nests of birds where you would never think of looking. There were times when he would show me a wren's nest or bullfinches or goldfinches and I would be right on top of the nest but still could not see it, but my dad could see it. He would show me where to look, explaining in great detail the clues I should be searching for to locate the nests. We would sit out of sight and see birds as they came in and out of the hedgerows. Watching as a bird sat on a branch and by following its movements through the foliage the bird would lead you right to its nest. But all of that took time and patience and one more very important aspect was needed if you were to stand any chance of seeing any wildlife in its own habitat, and that most important aspect was respect, respect for others, and respect for wildlife. I remember on his allotment my dad would be digging away and as he lifted a spade of soil you would hear him talking to a robin that kept jumping in the newly made hole in an attempt to catch a worm. Dad would be telling the robin that one of these days he would get himself buried if he wasn't careful!

So how does all this bird business help me in the RSPCA? Well one day a woman contacted me to say that she knew a man was keeping British birds and selling them without being 'closed ringed'. Right now then let me tell you about 'closed ringed'. If you breed a British bird, say a bullfinch, goldfinch, chaffinch, redpoll or linnet and intend to sell it you have to place on the bird's leg a specially made closed metal ring that can only be fitted whilst it is very young. The ring has to go over the bird's toes so that it sits around the leg. As the bird grows the toes get stronger making it impossible to get a closed ring on without injury to the bird. The idea being that if such a ring is found to be on a British-protected bird's leg then it's reasonable to assume that the ring was put on whilst the bird was still in the nest and also that the bird was bred in captivity and not taken from the wild. If a protected bird does not have a closed ring then it cannot be sold, offered for sale or used in barter.

Some keepers and breeders go to great lengths monitoring a nest discovered in the wild, keeping it under close observation waiting for just the right time to place closed rings on the newly hatched chicks so they can remove these wild birds, transferring them to their own aviaries. If it can be shown that they have the facilities to have bred such birds it makes it very difficult for anyone to detect what we call 'recently taken'. Some try and force the ring over the toes of the bird thus causing, in most cases, a lot of pain and suffering for the bird. Others go to the extent of placing a nail over one end of the closed ring and by gently hitting the nail they make the tampered end slightly larger, then by applying a little oil or grease they may be successful in getting the closed ring onto the leg. All these illegal methods of taking wild birds are very hard to detect and the eye of an expert ornithologist is needed: they look at the behaviour of the bird, how it appears in the aviary interacting with the other birds, they also look at its feathers and the colouration on the beak and legs. This is all very technical but that's what makes them good expert witnesses in court cases.

My informer lady told me that she, in fact, bred and kept British birds and through a friend of a friend had heard of a man who it was claimed was keeping British birds illegally. Having gleaned as much information from her as I could, I rang a colleague in the RSPCA who was classed as an expert witness with his experience in ornithology. After speaking with him it was decided that my informer would have to establish exactly what birds this man had. This could only be done if she visited him under the pretence that she wanted to purchase a British bird. She would then report back to me what she had seen. One Monday morning in 1971 she went to the address where she believed illegally caught British wild birds were being sold.

Later that same day she returned to my home where I was waiting with my colleague. Inside the house she had seen about eight bullfinches, four goldfinches, six siskins and about twenty redpolls. She added that all the birds had rings on but she could see that some of them were having difficulty in standing and perching. She also had seen blood on some of the birds' legs and some had disfigured toes. The man had told her that all the birds were for sale if she had the money. My informer then produced a cage containing a redpoll that she had just bought from the man. My colleague took this bird from the cage and examined the closed metal ring which he then removed from its leg without any effort.

Due to the complexity of this type of investigation I knew I would have to apply to the local magistrates for a search warrant that would authorise the search and removal of any evidence found. I took my findings to the local police and conferred with the police inspector who then assigned a sergeant to our team. My first hurdle was to convince the magistrates that I had enough evidence for them to grant a warrant. I appeared before the bench of magistrates and gave my evidence. Later that day I was granted the following warrant:

In the county of Leicester, Petty Sessional Division of Melton & Belvoir.

The information of Inspector John Norman of the Loughborough and North Leicestershire Branch of the RSPCA who upon oath states that he has reasonable grounds to suspect and does suspect that an offence against Section 6 of the Protection of Birds Act 1954 namely selling or offering for sale or having in possession for sale live wild birds being 8 bullfinches, 4 goldfinches, 6 siskins and about 20 redpolls included in the fourth schedule of the Protection of Birds Act 1954 has been committed by xxxxxx address xxxxxx and that evidence thereof may be found on the premises namely possession of recently taken birds.

Fully armed with this warrant we set off for the man's house. We had a brief meeting at the police station before setting out to make sure that all participants knew what their roles were going to be once inside the house: anyone seeing, or finding anything that may be of interest, or evidence, they would leave that item where it was found and bring it to my attention so that I could record those findings and where possible use the same as evidence. The sergeant and I went to the front door, also assisted by my colleague. Two police constables went around to the back door. The suspect opened the front door and on seeing us stood on his doorstep, his mouth opening wider than the door.

The sergeant introduced us all to the man and produced the search warrant. He then gave him a short explanation on what we intended doing. The man turned to the sergeant and said, "I'm not having all you bloody lot in here." The sergeant pointed out to the man that we were not looking for an invitation; the magistrates had already done that by issuing the warrant. He could either co-operate or be arrested and removed from the premises, the choice was his. The suspect then turned to me and said, "I haven't got any birds in the house." I

29

informed him that if that was the case we should be away in a very short time, and with that we entered his house.

On reaching the living room I could hear birds whistling. The noise came from different parts of the house. We went round all the rooms and in that house, with supposedly no birds, I found eleven bullfinches, twelve goldfinches, twenty-three redpolls but no siskins or any other species of protected birds. I also failed to find any instrument or item used for trapping wild birds. It seemed clear that although the man never admitted it, someone else had trapped these birds and he was only the seller. All the birds were seized and removed much to the disgust of the man who shouted, "I have never sold any of the birds." Little did he know, what I knew. The birds were taken to a place of safety and fully examined by my expert colleague. All the birds had metal closed rings but on examination you could clearly see where these rings had been tampered with to make them fit over the toes and onto the birds' legs. Some of the birds' legs were so badly damaged that they were referred to a vet who, after further examination gave evidence that in his opinion these birds had been caused unnecessary suffering.

At the end of my investigation I took out nine separate summonses against the man for 'unlawfully selling', 'unlawfully offering for sale', 'being in possession of live wild birds' and 'causing unnecessary suffering'. In the court the man pleaded guilty to the charges against him and he was fined. The birds that had been injured were re-homed under licence to recognised ornithologists. I then had the greatest pleasure, on recommendation of the court, of releasing the remaining birds back into the wild.

As a footnote to this chapter I give you the following information: whilst I was conducting the search of the man's house he picked up a bread knife and said to me, "This is going into your ribs the next time I see you!" The police sergeant warned the man about his behaviour and then asked me if I wanted to take the threat any further. I didn't as I felt the man's threat was made in the heat of the moment. Several weeks after the court case I was on duty in the local cattle market when I saw the man walking between the rows of farm produce. I stood to one side just out of sight of him and then as he came level with me I smacked him a good right-hander. He fell down to the ground, more from shock, I think, than the punch, but unfortunately in doing so he hit some egg crates and smashed a whole load of eggs.

A member of the public thought he had slipped and some helped him get back on his feet. He left the market ranting and raving about how he was going to get me done for hitting him, and lo and behold later that same day I was asked to call in at the local police station. There I spoke with a police inspector who informed me that the man had made an official complaint about my assault on him. The inspector said that in making enquiries about the man's claim he had been briefed by the sergeant who was witness to the threat of violence made by the man at the time of the search. The inspector told me that it had been agreed that the he was going to deal with the matter by having words with me. The inspector told me that he was not impressed with my action in the market, stating I should have known better and also pointing out that this action could have ruined my whole career. He made it quite clear that he was not happy with what I had done and gave me a right rollicking. Anyway I did not hear anything else about it and strangely I never saw the man again. By the way, I did have to pay for the three and a half dozen eggs that got broken.

CHAPTER 7

Stupidity

When I investigate cases of suspected cruelty I try and look at the offence with the degree of suffering being caused, and the offender's knowledge of that suffering. 'Mens rea' is the expression we use for guilty knowledge. Such was a case I was about to investigate. I was walking around one of the cattle markets in my branch area when I came across pen number 190. This pen was holding five sheep but I could see that one of the sheep, a ewe, was dead. Now let's get things into perspective, animals die. It is wrong to start running around the market making a scene because there is a dead animal. No matter where it is seen dead you must investigate and make your enquiries in a proper and orderly manner. So many of our inspectors have made a fool of themselves by saying or doing the wrong thing.

Members of the public will always look on a dead animal, especially in a cattle market, as 'someone must have been cruel'. Anyway I went into the pen and moved the dead ewe into an empty pen a few yards away. I did a quick examination of the ewe but could not see any obvious signs or reason for the death. I estimated, by examining the teeth, that she was about 4-5 years old, a little underweight but not what I would call offensive and its feet looked to be well trimmed. I found an old plastic sheet at the far end of the pens and used this to cover the ewe whilst I went to find the auctioneer. On speaking to him I was given the name of the person who had entered the ewe for sale. In fact the auctioneer told me that the sheep had already been sold about an hour ago and at that time all five sheep in the pen seemed to be in sound health. He then gave me the name of the farmer who had bought the sheep.

Making my way back to the pen I was stopped by a member of the public who wanted to tell me that they had seen a dead sheep in pen 190. What would I do without these informative people! I made all the right noises and assured this kind person that I was on the case and was making enquiries into the matter. On hearing this, my informer came out with the classic comment, "Some of these farmers want locking up!" See what I mean, they see a dead animal and someone has been cruel. I got a surprise when I got back to the pens as the four live sheep had been removed along with the dead one. Before I had time to wonder where they had gone I was told by one of the auctioneer's drovers that a man had loaded the four live sheep and the dead one onto a van and had driven off. The drover told me that although he did not know the man's name he had seen him many times before in the market and thought that he lived somewhere near Nottingham. But thanks to the auctioneer's cooperation I already had the man's details.

I made a telephone call to the man's farm and spoke to his good lady wife. I asked her if she would get her husband to ring me at the market as soon as he returned home. It was not long after that that my name was being broadcast over the public address system asking me to come to the main office. On the other end of the phone was the man who had removed the sheep. He told me he had purchased the five ewes and they seemed sound at the time but after returning from the paying office he found that one of the ewes was dead and someone had moved it into a separate pen and covered it up with a plastic sheet. I informed him of my involvement and asked if he had any idea how the ewe had died. He said that he didn't and was a bit upset that he had been told he must remove the carcass of the dead ewe. He stated that he had been told that unless he could prove that there had been some neglect by the auctioneer he would not be compensated for his loss. He had been told, "Buyer beware!" I asked the farmer if he would have a good look at the dead ewe and if he thought a vet should carry out a post-mortem that he would have to ring me again at the market. I did not have to wait long before I was again being asked on the public address system to report to the main office. Again I spoke to the farmer and he started thanking me for my persistence as on this second examination he had found something that even he was finding hard to believe. He stated that I should come over to his place right away and bring a vet. It never seems to amaze me how people think that I carry a vet in the back of

33

my van for such visits as this one.

Having called a vet who agreed to meet me at the farm a few miles outside the city of Nottingham, I found myself once again looking at the carcass of the ewe that I had seen earlier in the market. On this occasion though I was joined by the good vet. The farmer rolled the ewe over onto her back and parted the wool from around the belly. In unison the vet and I said, "God, I don't believe it!" The vet did a closer examination and told me that the ewe was five year old white-faced Leicester border cross ewe. The ewe had a septic vagina and its vulva had split open and someone had stitched her up with baler twine. The ewe had not received proper medical attention and the arteriole had perforated. The vet's opinion was that the ewe had been in considerable pain and that the suffering was completely unnecessary. The vet went on to say that the septic vagina would have been the main cause of death and that he would support me in any prosecution for causing that unnecessary suffering. I had been working with a lot of vets in the first few months as an inspector, but I had never seen one so incensed at what he had just seen. The vet said, "The person who did this took a piece of wire, tied a length of baler twine to the end of it and crudely stitched the poor sod up. It was not done yesterday; this was done many days ago. I can understand a farmer doing this as an outright emergency prior to it being seen by a vet, but to leave the ewe like this is beyond belief."

Later the same day I visited another farm and spoke to a man who admitted that he was the owner of the five ewes in pen 190. The recorded interview with this man went as follows:
Question: "Did you know that one of those ewes died whilst at the market?"
Reply: "No!"
Question: "Were they all in good health when they left this farm?"
Reply: "No, one had strained herself, I had to stitch her up."
Question: "How long ago was that?"
Reply: "About 3 weeks ago."

Question: "And what did you use for stitches?"
Reply: "Baler twine."
Question: "Did you have any veterinary surgeon to treat it?"
Reply: "No."
I told him of the vet's findings. Hearing this he replied, "I am sorry. I did not know it was suffering like that. I have 400 sheep and 200 beast and I would not harm any of them if I could avoid it." I informed this man that I would be reporting him for prosecution, and asked if there was anything else he wished to say. He replied, "I am sorry this has happened, I did not know she was suffering."
Question: "Would you like your own vet to examine the carcass so that he can give you an opinion?"
Reply: "No, if the vet who examined the ewe says she has suffered then I will respect his statement as a veterinary."

I took out two summonses against this farmer, they read as follows:

"That he did unlawfully cause unnecessary suffering to a certain animal, to wit a sheep, by unreasonably omitting to provide the same with proper and necessary care and attention, contrary to section 1, sub-section 1(a) of the Protection of Animals Act, 1911 as amended by the Protection of Animals (Amendment) Act 1954".

"That he did unlawfully cause unnecessary suffering to a certain animal, to wit a sheep by subjecting the same to an operation which was performed without due care or humanity, contrary to section 1, sub-section 1(e) of the Protection of Animals (Amendment) Act 1954".

The farmer pleaded guilty to the charges and was fined £20 with a further £15 to go towards the RSPCA costs.

Let me just reiterate a point on this case. Remember me giving you an explanation earlier regarding the difference between suffering and unnecessary suffering? Now look back to what the vet said about the stitching up of the ewe. He stated that he could understand a farmer doing this as an outright emergency prior to it seeing a vet. This vet was now applying that same lawful logic to what he was seeing, for the farmer to try and hold the ewe together for a few hours prior to it being attended by a vet could have been in certain circumstances acceptable, but the length of time the ewe had been suffering was, in his opinion, unnecessary.

The majority of farmers are very knowledgeable on their livestock's needs. Some hold, quite lawfully, various medicines and drugs prescribed by their veterinaries to treat and administer to their animals. Vets know their clients. They know who can and who cannot be trusted with such medicines and aids. Let's face it farmers in general are professionals dealing with livestock everyday. They have forgotten more than most will ever know. It's not in their interest to neglect an animal, or cause it unnecessary suffering, but unfortunately every now and again something like this case comes to light, and I think you will agree it can only be described as 'stupidity'.

CHAPTER 8

P.T.S

I had now been operating as an RSPCA inspector for one year and everything seemed to be going fairly well, but there is an area of my duties that I, at times, struggle with and that's the dreaded P.T.S. This is the abbreviation we use when we have to put an animal to sleep. All inspectors are highly trained in this field, but no amount of training can prepare you for this part of the job. I find that if I am carrying out this task on a severely injured animal, or an old dog that is in pain, then I get a feeling of satisfaction that I have been trained and have the skill to relieve that pain or suffering. The problem I face, and from what I hear so do my colleagues, is what do you do with a healthy unwanted animal? It's usually a cat or a dog or the litters of the same that cause this dilemma. It is so easy to say to the general public, "The RSPCA will not put a healthy animal to sleep." As an inspector I fully respect and endorse that statement but in reality what do I do? Let's try saying to the members of the public who are making these requests, "Go away! You try and find someone else, or another animal welfare society to help you. Or try and find homes yourself for those unwanted litters. Give them away to your neighbours and friends." What I am really saying is if I stick my head in the sand, when I pull it out all the problems will have gone away. Well every inspector in our Society knows that will not be the case, we know that within a few months those very animals will be producing their own unwanted litters; the older dogs running around in packs as stray dogs; colonies of feral cats appearing with feline diseases and infections, and due to their semi-wild state time has to be spent on trying to trap them. And if you are lucky enough to catch them you are back to the original question: what do you do with them?

I can tell you what I do in my branch. I have a centre that is open two nights a week giving the members of the public the chance to bring me their unwanted animals. On meeting the owners of such animals I try and give them some animal welfare education, such as spaying of females, and neutering of males and in lots of cases my branch offers financial assistance with the vet bills for these operations. Some of the animals can be taken in at local kennels where the RSPCA try and find new homes. Again in these cases those kennel fees have to be paid for. We always ask the person handing the animal over for a donation towards our costs, but far too often this is not given and the branch ends up paying those bills. Every RSPCA branch relies on the wonderful army of volunteers holding jumble sales, fêtes, manning shops, street collections, or any other way they can to raise sufficient money so that these bills can be paid. Don't forget the RSPCA receives no state aid. But after all our efforts and good intentions we are still left with unwanted animals that we are unable to find homes for.

It makes me so angry when I hear people criticizing the RSPCA when we have to produce figures that show that as a necessity we had to put to sleep a number of animals. I would like to bring to their attention that these animals were not bred by the RSPCA; they are not our animals. It's just that the RSPCA was doing its best for that animal and under the circumstances it ended up as one of the statistics of P.T.S.

I will now give you my statistics for the year ending 1970:

Dogs	P.T.S.	118
Dogs (under 6 weeks)	P.T.S.	47
Dogs	Found new homes	34
Cats	P.T.S.	197
Cats (under 6 weeks)	P.T.S.	19
Cats	Found new homes	15

Other animals (old or severely injured)

Guinea-pigs	P.T.S.	2
Swans	P.T.S.	2
Woodpigeons	P.T.S.	4
Wild birds (various)	P.T.S.	13
Wild rabbits	P.T.S.	5

The P.T.S figures above are the total figures for that year. The number of cats and dogs found new homes refers to the animals that I personally found a new home for without it having gone through the kennels. What the list does not show is the many cats and dogs that were found homes after being boarded for a short time in the kennels. Maybe you can now understand why I struggle with this side of my duties. One year ago I joined the RSPCA with the full intention of saving all animals from abuse and cruelty. I thought that single-handedly I was going to educate the whole country on animal welfare and yet here I am having to produce figures that show in one year I had to P.T.S 407 animals.

You know people often say to me after I have had to put an animal to sleep, "I bet you get used to it." I will tell you what I tell them, "The day I feel that I am getting used to it is the day I ask the RSPCA for my P45." No, I will never get used to it, in fact I never want to get used to it. What I will do is give every animal respect, and a dignified end to their lives.

CHAPTER 9

All is going well

Considering how far I had come over the past eighteen months things at home were going well. Peter was now two years old and Sandra was well aware that he had found his feet. The back garden at our house was some 100ft long with an old rickety wooden fence at the bottom. On the other side of this fence were the local allotments. Now Peter had found a new game to play with Sandra. It was called 'come and get me'. The rules of the game were simple: despite all my efforts to mend the fence Peter would find his way through it and would then stand on the allotment side just out of arm's length of Sandra. No amount of encouragement, bribes or threats of violence towards the sweet little boy would make him come just that little bit closer so that Sandra could pick him up and return him back into our garden. Not likely! Peter knew that his mam could neither get through the fence nor climb over it, although it was only a few feet high. He knew what his mam would have to do, and so did his mam. Mam had to run back to the house, go into the front street, run all the way around the block of houses and into the allotment, and guess what she found when she arrived? Yes, that's right, mummy's little boy had returned to the garden and was smiling from ear to ear at his mam. Sandra used to love every minute of this game. Well at least I think that's what she used to tell me. What Peter did not know was that he would soon have to share his mam's time and energy with a new playmate, as Sandra had just found out that she was expecting our second baby.

Like me, Sandra was still adjusting to our new way of life. One of the Society's criteria was that the wife of the inspector was not expected to go out to work. This was so they could answer the telephone when the inspector was not at home. You see if the inspectors' wives were at work then there would be no one to take the calls from the members of the public. They became one of the Society's greatest unpaid assets. They got to know every contact in the area and could give out information on animal welfare issues as good as, if not better than, most of the inspectors. This importance to the Society that the little ladies do not go out to work comes into this next story.

One of the ranks in the inspectorate was a 'travelling superintendent'. These officers had come through the ranks from inspectors and were now responsible for various regions of the country. They visited inspectors at their home to inspect their books and to make sure that the homes that were the property of the Society were properly maintained. They had the authority to sanction various DIY projects and would give permission for inspectors to claim out of pocket expenses that may have occurred whilst carrying out any authorised DIY or decorating. The superintendent would also visit the inspector out in the field, like at the cattle market, or just meet up with him at an arranged meeting point.

Due to their knowledge of the Society's policies and the general laws on animal welfare, he was a man we could turn to for advice and guidance. The majority of these superintendents were hard taskmasters who carried out their duty to the letter, and as they also had the power to take disciplinary action against inspectors who had fallen below the Society's standards it did make these officers, at times, unpopular. I had managed to keep on the right side of my travelling superintendent so far, but a couple of incidents took place that made me smile.

My superintendent came to see me at my house and asked me where I was the previous Thursday between 1.30p.m. and 2.30p.m. Now for the life of me I could not remember, but as all inspectors keep a very detailed notebook it did not take me long to produce mine and explain to him where I was on that said date and time. After reading my pocket notebook he asked me if I knew where my wife was on that day and at that time. Please note that he did not say Sandra, but your wife. They always adopted a standoffish attitude, a kind of them and us. It was as if they were afraid of becoming familiar with the inspector. I suppose it was that old adage 'familiarity breeds contempt' and no way could these

41

officers have a contemptuous inspector. Anyway I asked him what was the reason for knowing where my wife was. He duly informed me that if my wife could confirm her whereabouts, then all would be revealed. I called Sandra into the room. Again please note that I called her into the room, as wives were not expected to be privy to conversations between inspectors and superintendents.

Sandra entered and was asked the same question regarding the date and time. As our wives were not expected to keep a notebook it took some time for her to come up with an answer. "Yes, I remember, last Thursday was the last Thursday of the month and that's the day I take Peter to the children's clinic for his check up." Having solved the mystery the superintendent then revealed his reason for this visit. A member of the public had phoned around that time last Thursday and failed to get an answer. In frustration they had then phoned the RSPCA HQ in London to complain that they were unable to speak to the RSPCA in Loughborough, as there was no one answering the phone. Sandra and I both looked at each other with a smile, both thinking that her explanation was quite a valid reason for not being at the end of the phone on the day and time given. How wrong could we have been! The superintendent then told us the Society's remedy that would solve any future upset of the public. That remedy was simple, Sandra was told to change the clinic times so that it fitted in with a time that I would be at home to take any calls.

If you think that was a good story then try this next one. A few months later the manhole cover in our backyard overflowed. Now this manhole served about five houses, and was the junction point for the main sewage drainage system. I contacted the RSPCA Property Department and told them of the emergency and they promptly authorised me to contact a workman to attend to the offending drain. Within a short time a man came, made his inspection, and said that the drains were well and truly blocked with sewage but it would not be long before he would have the problem sorted. True to his word after a push and pull on a few drain rods everything in the garden smelt sweet again.

As the junction was taking sewage from around five houses the man said it was impossible to say who had caused the blockage, but as it was on the RSPCA's property he would have to leave the bill for his work with me. So far so good I hear you all say. I hope you have not forgotten my travelling superintendent. Over he comes having been informed by the Property Department that there would be a bill for him to sign as a job completed satisfactorily. I gave him an update on what I had seen that caused me to contact the Property Department and what the drain man had told me about it being impossible to lay blame on any one of the houses that this manhole served. But we had forgotten that an RSPCA travelling superintendent was a man of knowledge in all trades. He asked if he could have a word with the wife, and on seeing her he asked her what type of toilet paper we used. Sandra as seriously as she could, informed him, and on hearing this he gave Sandra two different brand names of a more favourable toilet paper, and requested that she change to one of them. Well did she? You will have to ask her when you see her.

CHAPTER 10

Piggy in the middle

No, this is not about a pig, although some will say it is because the piggy is me. I was a police special constable before I joined the RSPCA. I left the Specials after my successful exam results had sent me to Loughborough. As I was saying 'piggy in the middle', although I had settled down very nicely in my new role, and Sandra and Peter were just fine, things were happening within my branch that at times made me feel uneasy. Those wonderful volunteers that gave up their time to raise money for the Society and the ones that formed the local branch committee did not all see eye to eye. In my branch I had some first-rate people. Our local vet was a member of the branch committee and what a help he was, not only from a vet's point of view, but from his understanding of the difficulties inspectors have at times in trying to carry out their duties. I will always be indebted to the chairman of our branch. Her name was the 'Baroness Van-de-Feltz'. She was a lady in every sense of the word. She spoke direct, no side talk or behind your back. She was genuinely concerned about the inspector and his family. She campaigned staunchly with the RSPCA HQ regarding bringing in new ideas that would improve the inspector's standard of living. Some committee members wanted to go one way, and others that were more set in their ways wanted to remain as they were. I suppose it's the same in all walks of life when you have a group of people all wanting what they feel is best for their pet subject.

You see the RSPCA branch spends their raised monies, as they feel best. They have to contribute annually to HQ for the inspectorate's work and all the administrations that they use within the Society. Once they had made their annual subscription, they were a power unto themselves. In my branch if things started to get a little bit messy, or politically incorrect then it was poor old me who was 'piggy in the middle' and had to sort things out, with one committee member telling me to do one thing and another asking me to do the total opposite.

Well it all started to get a little out of hand and at several meetings personnel from HQ were present. I was getting the old 'wink and nod' from several people who were advising me to ask for a transfer, but this was alien to me. Why should I want to leave? Anyway one meeting led to another and in a very short period of time it was clear to me that I just had to get out of this situation. I had spoken to a number of my bosses at HQ and all seemed to be saying the same thing: to stick it out a bit longer and see what happens; that it was nothing do with the way I was carrying out my work. Well I took their advice and let the committee members sort things out in their own good time. My work was still as hectic as ever, like getting the local police to stop the traffic in the middle of Loughborough on a busy Saturday afternoon, much to the delight of everyone, as I escorted a female mallard and her nine newly hatched family over the road and into a park lake.

More cruelty cases to investigate. You know, I get so much pleasure out of this side of my work, especially after all the hard work, and endless hours putting the evidence together, getting into the court and hearing the magistrate saying, "we find this case proved." It's all part of trying to put that word 'prevention' in the Society's name into operation. I might not have got there early enough to prevent that animal suffering, but when the cases are well covered by the media and the newspapers, it is hoped that it will deter someone else from going down that same road.

CHAPTER 11

Transfer

It was now early June 1972, and I had been waiting on tenterhooks for notification that I might be transferred to another branch, and that could be anywhere in England or Wales. Since the various committee meetings I had taken advice from some very senior officers at HQ. I had made it clear that if my being moved would help the Society solve any of their problems by not having an inspector in that branch to worry about, then Sandra and I were willing to be transferred regardless of the fact that Sandra was some eight months pregnant. We had stated, jokingly, that as long as she did not give birth in the back of the furniture van then we would leave it up to HQ to sort out a removal date. We opened the envelope from HQ as if it contained a letter bomb, little by little lifting up the flap, wanting to know if our new posting was inside, but in another way not wanting to know. Bingo, there it was, the official instruction, it read:

On Thursday 29th June 1972, the Society requires you to be transferred to Haverfordwest, where you will serve the Pembrokeshire branch of the RSPCA (notice how the instruction stated 'you' with no mention of the family). "Haverfordwest", said Sandra, "where on earth is that?" "In Pembrokeshire," I said, "I've heard of that but where is it?" said Sandra. "Don't know," I replied. I went and got out the road map of Great Britain. We went through the index: Haverfordwest, Pembrokeshire, and South Wales. "Wales," we both said in unison. Now we had heard of Wales and we started to look at the map of the area: Fishguard, St David's, Milford Haven, Tenby, Saundersfoot, and mile after mile of coastline as well as upland areas called 'Prescelly Mountains'.

We went to the local stationery store in town and purchased whatever they had on Pembrokeshire. One was a guidebook with photographs of some of the places I have just mentioned and we could see lovely beaches, towns and villages. We could not believe our luck! That instruction could have read any one of a hundred or more of the Society's branches but there in black and white it said Haverfordwest, Pembrokeshire. We telephoned our mams and dads to give them the good news, and on hearing the location their reaction was the same as ours "Haverfordwest, where is that?" On telling them, as we were both experts on the area by now, they started booking their next summer holidays.

Over the next few days Sandra started to pack our belongings into tea chests once again, and on this occasion a more experienced Peter helped her. I had to say my goodbyes to various people, but my biggest surprise was from the farmers at Melton Mowbray Cattle Market. Despite the fact that I had at least three prosecutions under my belt resulting from beasts I found to be neglected and suffering, it seems the auctioneers and the farmers in general had appreciated my vigilance as they had clubbed together and I was presented with a state of the art portable tape recorder, and the farmer who made the presentation was Henry (remember Henry?). Some of the lads had recorded their own personal farewell messages on the tape, and believe me some of those so-called goodbyes were not for delicate ears, but I do believe they were all given, joking apart, with the same feeling that I had about leaving.

The Society does not grant any time off work for an inspector to visit his new station, not even for the good wife to see what she might need in new curtains, carpets etc, or for us to visit the local school, or even make contact with a doctor. Don't forget Sandra's condition. No, if you required to make any such arrangements then that was done in your own time, and at your own expense. The inspector had his instructions from HQ. You would arrange for two estimates for the removal to be sent to HQ, they would then inform the inspector which of those removal firms had been engaged in the transfer, and the inspector then contacted that firm to arrange times of collection. Easy, why should anyone be concerned about moving into a house that they had never seen, to an area they knew nothing about? I wonder why anyone would want to worry about such trivial things.

Thursday 29th June 1972, Sandra and Peter were with me in my van travelling towards Wales. Sandra, with the road map on her lap, was giving me the left, right and straight on instructions. The furniture van was going to start out later and we had estimated that it should arrive a couple of hours after us. I parked my van on top of a plateau reached by roads that had wound up the hill from the main road. We sat and looked over the town of Haverfordwest. It looked great. We had seen the valleys and Prescelly Mountains as we had crossed from Carmarthen down into Haverfordwest. I thought that, as we sat at the end of Queensway, the road that our new home was on, with a bit of luck we could be here for the next seven years.

We opened the front door of our new home and Peter started his own exploration of the various rooms, closely followed by the two of us. "Not bad, not bad at all," said Sandra. "A bit of decorating to give it that personal touch and it will be O.K." There was a good-sized back garden for Peter to play in and to Sandra's delight a good strong fence to prevent anymore 'come and get me' games. Whilst we were waiting for the furniture van we met our new neighbours. Marion and John along with Marion's mum lived on one side and Ann and Charles lived on the other side. Where our garden joined with the house at the bottom side of the street was a Mr and Mrs Thomas, he being the Chief Superintendent at the local police station. Now that was handy I thought.

Marion had made tea and cakes for us, and within a very short time the furniture van arrived and it was 'all hands to the pumps'. Due to the 'enormous' amount of items we owned the van was unloaded and gone within half an hour. HQ gave us plenty of time to settle into our new home and get things sorted out. We moved on a Thursday, I was on duty the next Monday. As I said plenty of time to settle in!

My first few days were spent in rather the same way as my first days in

Loughborough, with Sandra doing the same, but priority was given to finding a good family doctor. I had reminded her to make sure that she had the baby at a time that I was available to answer the phone in her absence! I don't remember exactly what her reply was but it sounded something like 'four cobs'.

On Monday 10th July, I had some calls to make in the Tenby area and Sandra and Peter came along for the ride, as they had not yet been to many of the coastal towns. One of the beaches we visited that day was at Manorbier. We all went for a walk along the beach and Peter splashed in and out of the sea trying to get as wet as he could before Sandra saw him. But Sandra had her mind on other things. She stopped and held her stomach and said, "I think we should be getting home." I said, "What, now?" Sandra replied, "Right now!" By the time we arrived home it seems our new baby had liked the idea of living in Wales as it was trying to make an entry as we walked in the front door. Sandra sat on the bottom step of the stairs and waited for the ambulance, and in no time at all she was on her way to the hospital. In the early hours of Tuesday 11th July 1972 Sara Adela, Peter's little sister came into our world.

On telling our travelling superintendent of our new arrival he congratulated me and gave me permission to carry out only emergency duties over the next two days. Who said these men have no hearts?

CHAPTER 12

Oil pollution

With my area covering some 190 miles of coastline I was becoming more and more experienced in the field of oil pollution. The thick crude oil that lay in small pockets in various coves was a constant nightmare. There did not have to be a reported spillage, these coves along the Pembrokeshire coastline held lots of their own little oil slicks and these were dispersed whenever there was a high tide and a rough sea covering any unsuspecting seabirds. Most of these birds were diving birds so if the oil did not get onto them when they entered the sea it would more than likely get them on the way out. I would walk along these hidden coves and come across many sea birds stranded on the beach, unable to open their wings due to the thick black crude oil. Petroleum oil would affect other birds. It coated the birds' feathers in an oily mass with the secondary infliction of burning the skin of the bird, making it more deadly than the crude oil. It was not always the amount of oil on the bird that resulted in its death or survival but the amount of oil the bird had swallowed.

It was essential that as soon as I came across a bird that I thought would stand a chance of being cleaned up I would place an elastic band around its bill preventing the bird from trying to preen itself. The RSPCA has, in Somerset, one of the best oil pollution cleaning centres in the world, and the highly trained staff at this centre had a lot of success with birds and other wildlife. It had been shown that the first action taken by the person finding the polluted bird was vital to the potential survival of that bird. For many years we had been attempting to clean the majority of the oil away from the birds before taking them to the centre but our expert knowledge had now found that the most important task was to prevent the further ingestion of oil into the bird's stomach. If the birds could be taken to our centre, or into the care of one of our many trained inspectors, of which I was one, then the bird would have a greater chance of survival. I was collecting a wide range of seabirds but mainly guillemots, gannets and razorbills, the latter being the emblem of the Pembrokeshire National Parks.

RSPCA Inspector John Norman with oil pollution victims
Photograph: Courtesy of The Western Telegraph

I also had to deal with the affect of pollution on young seal pups. Again many different methods of cleaning had been tried, some were more successful than others and as with the birds the main problem was ingestion. I was working very closely with the Pembrokeshire National Park wardens, and we heard from a local fisherman that he had seen a number of seals on the island of Skomer, just off the coast from St David's. I was asked to go along with two of the wardens and we spent three days on this uninhabited piece of Wales.

Our aim was to try out new methods of cleaning the seal pups. What we found in the past was that even if we managed to clean up a seal pup whilst it was still on the beach the moment its parent returned to it the oil from the parent would re-contaminate the pup. So we set about finding ourselves a nice little bay with a few oiled pups, and that did not take more than an hour on our first day of searching. As we came onto the coves the parents all scrambled back into the sea leaving the pups very conveniently on the beach. First of all we scooped out a rut in the sand along the same line that the parent seal had taken when coming in and out of the sea attending to their offspring. We then poured diluted oil cleaner into this area so that when the parent returned to the pup using this route it would help to clean off the oil. In the past we would spend a long time trying to clean the pup's entire coat, but again it had been found that as long as we cleaned only a small area of the coat, preferably along its back, this would enable the seal to shed that coat in the natural way. It is similar to the part in the film *Goldfinger*, when he painted the girl gold. He should have left a small area for her skin to breathe. Well that's just what we were doing.

We had applied a mild hand cream to the pup's mouth, lips, eyes and nostrils and instead of upsetting it unnecessarily by cleaning the whole of its coat we just kept one small area free of oil. The method described was carried out on about fifty pups over the next few days. To our great delight none died whilst we were at the island and also none were abandoned by their parents, as unfortunately so often happens after interference by humans. The local fishermen who were asked to keep a close eye on the seals made comments that they saw the pups later shedding their coats and none appeared the worse for our intervention. A report complete with before and after photographs of our work was sent to various organisations that specialized in the welfare of seals, and our actions were repeated many times by other organisations.

CHAPTER 13

I've got to save the sheep

Due to the high cliffs around the Pembrokeshire coastline I found myself carrying out more and more rescues of animals that for one reason or another found themselves stranded down these cliffs. One such rescue was on Saturday, 2nd December 1972, I found myself peering down from the top of a 200ft cliff. I was crouched against the pelting rain, cupping my ear. Somewhere far below I could hear the plaintive bleating of frightened sheep. Their sound was barely audible above the roaring sea that was pounding the coast below me. I could see two sheep; they looked like hardy Welsh cross Leicester borders. I had been told by Mr Calella, the farmer who owned the sheep, that they had been chased by a dog, separated from the flock, and panic stricken, they had crashed through a fence and leapt blindly over the edge of the cliff.

Miraculously, loose shale had broken their fall and now they were on a narrow ledge a few feet wide about 150ft down. I could see that a third sheep had plummeted to its death as it lay on the wave lashed rocks below. I knew I only had to contact the local coastguard or even the fire brigade as they would only be too willing to help, but it wouldn't have been fair. I always feel that their job is the preservation of human life. As an RSPCA inspector, animals were my responsibility and anyway I was miles away from a proper road. The teams that would have helped would, like me, have had to walk some distance to the cliff edge and if those organisations were needed elsewhere, how would I feel knowing that I had tied them up on this job. No, this was one for me. After all I did have the farmer with me. He was a very able and willing helper so I decided that at least the initial stages of the rescue we could do on our own. "Get me my rope from the van," I asked Mr Calella, "I'm going over." We hitched the rope around a very sturdy fence post, tied it around my waist, using all the knots I had been shown at training school. Mr Calella took the strain of the rope and lowered me down the cliff face. Every movement of the rope sent down showers of stones. A couple of times I found myself swinging giddily into space, as I had to kick away from the cliff face. The unrelenting rain seemed to have a personal grudge against me, as I was soaked to the skin.

On reaching the two sheep they both lifted their bedraggled heads and baa-ed at me. I'm sure one of them said, "You must be mad!" As I moved towards the tiny ledge that they were standing on, one of the sheep leapt at me, butting me in the chest. My reflexes were quick enough to grab the sheep and hold it against the cliff face. The sheep violently struggled and we both swung out into space. As we crashed back into the cliff face another shower of shale and stones came pelting down. I was praying that the rope would last and the good farmer would be strong enough to hold on. I pinned the sheep against the cliff with my body and tried to take a breather. It was then that I saw a gully, it was no more than a tiny cranny but clearly it must lead to the top of the cliff.

If only, I thought, I could get the two sheep to use this as their way of escape. I managed to return the frightened sheep back onto the ledge, and shouted up to the farmer that I wanted to be pulled back up to the cliff top. I told Mr Calella about the gully and took him to the edge of the cliff to point it out to him, but on looking over the edge my hopes were dashed, the gully was blocked with old fencing and yards of wire. This was why the sheep had been unable to use the route themselves. "Alright," I said, "lower me over again, I'll try and clear that damn gully." I disentangled the wire, pulled the fence post apart and flung the lot into the sea below. I then swung out off the face of the cliff into space and dropped in behind the two sheep doing everything I could to encourage the sheep to go towards the gully but to no avail. Once again I came back to the top of the cliff.

I had been at this rescue for nearly three hours, my hands were painfully sore and the rest of me was very tired, cold and very, very wet.

I discussed the situation with my farmer friend and he agreed with my idea that if I was to go back down the cliff armed with some turnip scraps and lay a trail along the gully the two sheep may just feed off them and find their way back to safety. So I went down again and on returning told the farmer, "Let's hope that they have the sense to follow their noses!"

We both left the scene and I made arrangements to return the next day to see what progress had been made. On pulling up in the farmyard the next morning one happy farmer said, "It worked, Inspector Norman, it worked!" He took me into the lower field that led down to the rescue site and pointed out the two sheep, back with the rest of the flock, none the worse for their ordeal.

It is part of the inspector's duties to put in a rescue report, especially if a member of the public is involved. I was honoured to receive from the Society a framed certificate of merit for my work. The citation read 'For his courage and determination in rescuing two sheep'. Mr Calella also received one as well, and that really pleased me.

CHAPTER 14

Brothers in Arms

I was visited by my brother Barry and his family. They were spending a week's holiday with us in Haverfordwest. During this time Barry asked me about the possibilities of him becoming an inspector. Barry had shown a great interest in my work since I had started and like me had a passion for working with animals. I gave him all the information and encouraged him to apply for a position, as I knew he had the qualities required. As with my application, the ball started rolling and in 1973 we stood side by side in the same uniform having our photographs taken, advertising to the world that they now had two Normans to deal with if they wanted to abuse or neglect animals. Our mam and dad could not believe it, both of their sons in uniform, both inspectors in the RSPCA. They told everyone they met for years afterwards, they were so proud of us. If either one of us had had a story in the paper they had a copy in their own scrapbook and if either one of us appeared on the television it would make their day.

Barry served in Wolverhampton and then was transferred to Carmarthen just a few miles away from Haverfordwest. Barry was a good officer and made a reputation for himself as a conscientious, dedicated inspector. Sadly on the 23rd April 1986, aged just 44 years, Barry suffered a massive heart attack and died. He had served the Society for 15 years and was sadly missed. You can imagine how Mam and Dad took it; Dad was recovering from a heart attack himself and Mam suffered from angina. Hearts were not the best organs in our family. No parent expects to bury their children and this event silenced the Normans' usual outgoing, joyous outlook on life for a long, long time.

The Norman Brothers, Barry (left) and John (right)

CHAPTER 15

Agricultural livestock

I met many farmers in my work as a RSPCA inspector and they were very professional people but like all aspects of our society there are those amongst us that let the profession down. This was so in the following case, which began with a tip off.

I was told that if I were to visit a certain farm I would find some dead calves, and some that, although alive, were in need of veterinary attention. As I would be going onto agricultural land I made the visit assisted by a vet, who had no connection with the farm, and a local police officer who, although he knew the farmer, neither he nor his colleagues had had any dealings with him.

The farm was located down an unmade track at the back of beyond, miles away from any other properties. It was clear as we drove into the farmyard that this establishment was run down and not being managed properly. At 10.00a.m. the three of us stood outside the farmhouse. The police officer did the customary knock on the front door but after a short while, as there was no response, we went for a walk around the farm to try to locate some human life. Around the back of one of the many barns I saw the bloated carcass of a young calf. The vet took a quick look at it and stated that it was a calf about three months of age, which, because of its bloated condition, had been dead for a few days. We went inside the nearest outbuilding and were overpowered by a smell. It was that smell that stays with you for years. Any person who has had the misfortune to smell a dead, rotting body, human or animal will know exactly what I mean.

There were several other bloated carcasses of calves, in various degrees of decomposition, in some cases no more than the skeleton remained. The buildings had not been cleaned out in months and the slurry was running under the doors and out into the farmyard. To our surprise, amongst all this there were three live calves. I went further inside the building to drive them towards the vet. As they turned to face me I could not believe what I was looking at. These poor animals' faces were completely covered in a scaly crust. Other parts of their bodies were also infested, and I recognized this as ringworm. This is common in young cattle especially if, like these calves, they are kept indoors without having any natural light or sunshine on them.

The poor animals' faces were covered in a scaly crust.

I also found three other calves alive in a second building; again all were in the advanced state of ringworm. The police officer went out into the yard leaving the vet and me to make notes and take photographs. We could hear the officer walking around the various buildings calling out the name of the farmer in an attempt to locate him. I was hoping that if the farmer did show his face the officer would keep his cool. We found a clean area in one of the buildings and bedded the six calves down. In thirty years as a veterinary surgeon it was the worst case of ringworm the vet had ever seen. He also said that what made him more angry was that one of the best treatments for ringworm was completely free of charge to the farmer - sunlight. It was now May, and if these calves had been exposed to a little bit of sunlight each day, along with the general treatment they should have been given, then the calves would not have been in this sorry state. The vet had no hesitation in giving me his opinion that these calves were being caused unnecessary suffering.

We decided to go back to the police station, contact the agent for the Ministry of Agriculture, and then return to the farm later in the day. The vet, the police officer and two of his colleagues plus two officers from the Ministry of Agriculture were going to assisting me. We arrived back at the farm, this time fully prepared. I went to the front door of the farmhouse with the police officers and they knocked a couple of times but again there was no reply. We took the new recruits over to the buildings where the carcasses were. The men from the Ministry took it in their stride, but one of the police officers showed us what he had had for his breakfast that morning. They were shown the calves with ringworm and the officers from the Ministry reiterated what the vet had said about what a difference a little bit of sunshine would have made.

As we all made our way through the yard I looked towards the farmhouse and saw a woman come out of the front door, pick up a box from the side and go back indoors. My mouth fell open but no sound came out. I pointed to the house and I heard one of the police officers say, "I don't believe that." "What?" asked the vet, "There's somebody in the house," replied the officer. "Don't talk daft," said his mate. "Yes", I managed to say, "I've just seen a woman come out, then go back in." We all broke into a run down the yard. I don't know why we did that; it just seemed the thing to do. On reaching the front door one of the police officers gave a knock, you know the one I mean, the one that makes the back door rattle. We all took one step back and waited. Everybody does that don't they; they knock on the door, and then take one step back. Anyway as calm as you like the woman opened the front door. She looked at the seven of us and said, "What?" "What?" said the police officer who had been with me since 10.00a.m. "How long have you been in the house?" "All day, I've just got out of bed," she replied. "It's five in the afternoon," said one of the other police officers. The first officer seemed to collect himself and informed the woman as to who we all were and our interest in the farm animals.

The woman told us that her partner, the farmer, had gone into Carmarthen earlier that morning and would not be back until after midnight, so if we had any questions we would have to come back in the morning. The vet informed her that the calves needed attention and that, in his opinion, they were suffering. She replied that there was nothing wrong with the animals and that they would be all right. I asked her who was responsible for the animals' welfare. She replied that it was her partner and that she had nothing to do with any of the animals. She then closed the door and despite our talking through the letterbox she refused to say anymore or show her face.

We all returned to the outbuildings taking more photographs, preparing notes and making arrangements for the various treatments that the calves would need. Also a full log was made of the unburied carcasses. I was assisting these officers, moving from one building to the other when I just happened to glance at the farmhouse, and I swear I saw a man's face at one of the bedroom windows. I beckoned for one of the police officers to come over to where I was standing inside the building, and in true 'James Bond style' we peered through a crack in the outbuilding's window and the police officer saw, yes, you've guessed it, nothing. He asked, "Are you sure?" "As sure as you were when you saw the woman earlier on," I replied. With that he calmly walked over to the other officers. They in turn spoke to the Ministry men and everyone then ended up in my building. The plan of action was that we would go to the house, one police officer and a Ministry man would go to the back door and the rest of us would knock on the front door and see who would come and answer it.

The police officer gave a gentle tap on the door, yes it was only a gentle tap, and within seconds a man opened it. The police officer recognised him as the farmer and said to him, "Where have you just come from?" "Upstairs," replied the man. The officer asked, "Have you been upstairs all the time?" "Yes," he replied, "I saw the RSPCA man and somebody else looking around the farm this morning so I thought I would keep out of the way." The police officer and his colleagues spoke at length to the man, and after a while he agreed to accompany us around the farm. On reaching the first bloated carcass I asked, "What happened to this calf?" He replied, "It must have died before it got here." I asked, "Did you put it here after it died?" He replied, "No it died here." This incomprehensible attitude towards the state of his farm and animals was about as far as we got with him. I told him that I would be reporting him for prosecution for failing to provide the proper and necessary care and attention to the six calves that we found alive. The Ministry reported him for several offences relating to unburied carcasses and not keeping proper records of livestock.

Over the next few weeks I made several visits back to the farm to check on the calves and they had all responded well to the veterinary treatment and they were looking a lot better. I was unable to bring charges regarding the dead calves due to lack of evidence from the vets as to how they died. (Remember what I told you about having to provide veterinary evidence to prove a case; well this was one of those frustrating times.) The farmer pleaded guilty to the charges laid. He was fined but not disqualified from keeping any animals. After the court case he was often visited by the Ministry and given advice in cleaning up his farm by the Ministry's Farm Animal Welfare Department. I can also report to you that the woman at the farm admitted to me later in the investigation that she did have some responsibility for the animals' welfare. She was also charged and found guilty of all the offences.

CHAPTER 16

Several cases

Over the previous year I had to deal with some very difficult cases, like the minister who neglected his flock; yes, that's what he did. The newspapers loved giving that title to the case every time they wrote about it. I went to inspect some goats that were being kept by a minister in a field close to his parish church. He had failed to notify a vet when one of his goats became lame due to a severe injury, and a second goat was found to have been suffering for many days with severe mastitis. Both goats had to be destroyed owing to their condition and two others were re-homed. The minister pleaded guilty to the two charges. He stated that he had asked a local farmer three days before my visit to look at the goats and tell him if he thought the goats needed to see a vet. Up to the time of my visit the farmer had not seen the goats. The minister had not attended to his goat with mastitis. In his statement he said, "I think I should have done."

On another investigation I interviewed a man about a dog I had found dead close to a railway line. On examination I could see that it had been stabbed many times in various parts of its body. I took the carcass of the dog to a vet who said that he had found the dog to have fifteen wounds, all consistent with a long-bladed knife. The vet went on to say that his post-mortem examination had revealed that only one of these wounds would have caused a quick death as this had gone through the heart, all the other wounds had caused some damage to organs but in the main these had caused only internal bleeding. The vet also stated that only if evidence could be provided to support the fact that the heart wound was not the first stabbing then, and only then, would he be able to support a case of causing unnecessary suffering. In other words if the person responsible for this act stated that the first stab went into the heart then the vet would have to say that dog was then dead and any other stabbings after that were inconsequential.

I did interview the owner of the dog and the interview record read as follows:

Question: "Do you own a mongrel dog?"

Reply: "Yes, its mine. I know what you have come about."

Question: "The dog has got several stab wounds on its body consistent with knife wounds."

Reply: "That's right I did it. I took the dog down by the train lines and killed it."

Question: "Why?"

Reply: "The landlord told me I had to get rid of the dog so I killed it myself. I stabbed it with a bread knife but I don't know how many times."

Question: "Can you tell me where on the dog you first stabbed it?"

Reply: "No, I just stabbed it in its body."

Question: "What do you mean in the body?"

Reply: "The stomach part."

Question: "Did you stab the dog through the left side of the ribcage?"

Reply: "Yes, but not till it lay on the ground squealing, then I stabbed it in the ribs."

As you can see the man by his own admission stated that the dog did not die from the first stab wound therefore the vet was able to give his support that this man "did cause the dog unnecessary suffering by unreasonably killing it in an improper manner". The man later pleaded guilty to the charge and along with a fine and costs was given a disqualification order preventing him from owning a dog for the next five years.

Another case came to my attention; a member of the public contacted me to say that that if I was to go to a certain point in the docks and look down the side of one of the wooden pier supports I would see, just under the waterline, something that might interest me. With this the telephone at the other end went dead. It is not unusual for RSPCA inspectors to get such telephone calls. It seems that the member of the public had seen or heard something that they thought was wrong and they just had to pass whatever information they had onto us. I was very grateful of any information no matter how it was obtained, but it does make it very difficult at times if we have not got enough of the jigsaw to make a full picture. We never disclose from whom we obtain our information so remember, my dear friends, leave me with some contact number, in case I have to contact you again to clarify a point. Take this call for instance. If I had not been able to locate the very point stated by the anonymous caller, then the following information I am about to give you may have been undetected and left the caller wrongly thinking that the RSPCA had not followed up on their call.

It was Thursday, 29th May 1975 and I was at the docks looking for the location as indicated by the anonymous telephone call. I had seen three fishermen at the end of the pier. They asked what I was looking for. Now these locals knew more about the area than me so I told them of my search and despite what they might find they put down their rods and agreed to help me in the search. After a very short time one of the men shouted out. I cannot print the words he shouted out but it was sufficient enough for me to know he had found what I was looking for. At the end of the pier down by the side of a wooden support I could see just under the waterline the distinctive shape of a dog's body. I climbed over various wooden beams, and I was able to get over the top of the body and pull it out of the water and bring it onto dry land.

The dog was a black female Labrador of adult age and it seemed to have been in good bodily condition. On seeing the dog on dry land one of the fishermen with me seemed to think that he had seen this dog before or at least as he said a dog that looked just like it. He knew the town and the street but not the number of the house where he had seen the dog. He claimed to have seen a man walking with this dog. He told me which street it was and armed with this information I placed the carcass of the dog in the rear of my van, covered it with a blanket and drove the short distance to the place mentioned. I knocked on several doors in the street asking people if they knew of anyone in the area who owned a black female Labrador-type dog.

Several people indicated that they thought they had seen one about but could not direct me to a specific house. I had already decided that I would not at this point contact the local newspapers as I felt that if the perpetrators got wind that I was on the lookout for them, they would get a nice little story together, which I did not want. This dog had been drowned and whoever carried out that deed of cruelty now had one very calm, cool and collected RSPCA inspector looking for them, and if you believe that description of me then you have not read the other chapters in this book. You know I just love it when I arrive unexpected and unannounced on their doorstep and I say, "Hello, sorry to disturb you, my name is Inspector Norman of the RSPCA. Do you own a dog?" The look on the face of those who have committed acts of cruelty, who thought their secrets were safe, that look is priceless.

Well, lo and behold there I was. The door was being opened by a man and I said, "Hello, sorry to disturb you, my name is Inspector Norman of the RSPCA. Do you own a dog?" The man replied, "No." I asked, "Did you own a dog?" "Yes," said the man, "but I gave it away to a man in Swansea." I asked, "When did you give the dog away?" He replied, "a few weeks ago." I asked, "What type of dog was your dog?" "A black lab," said the man. Now from what I was feeling and hearing I was sure that this was my man. Several of the people in the street had pointed this house out as one of the houses that had a black Labrador. I invited the man to come over to the rear of my van and look at the carcass of the dog. On seeing it he said, "Yes, that's mine, I told you a lie about it going to a man in Swansea." I gave this person a caution and asked him if he had put the dog in the water, and he replied, "Yes, I did it. I could not afford to feed her. I took her to the pier tied a sack of stones around her neck and chucked her into the sea." I asked him when he carried out this act. He replied, "It was about a week ago."

I then completed my interview with this person and after obtaining all the details I required I informed him that I would be reporting him for causing unnecessary suffering to that dog. Later that same day I had the dog examined by a vet who stated after the post-mortem examination that the dog had died from drowning and it would have taken some four minutes to die. There were no other signs of illness or internal ruptures and he concluded his report by saying that the dog had been caused considerable unnecessary suffering.

The offender pleaded not guilty to the charge and that he caused the dog unnecessary suffering by unreasonably killing it in an improper manner. He told the magistrate that he had committed the act at 2.15a.m. as there was no one about and this was the best time to do it. He said, "After tying the sack of stones around the neck of the dog I put it over the edge of the pier and it went right down. I looked for a while to make sure it did not come up. I saw bubbles but nothing else." When the man was asked by the RSPCA prosecuting solicitor if it had occurred to him that the dog would suffer, the man replied, "I did not think it would suffer for long." When asked why he had not taken the dog to the veterinary surgeon that was located at the end of his street, he replied, "That would have cost money wouldn't it?" The man then denied that he drowned the dog in the middle of the night because he knew it was wrong and he refused to say why he had lied to me about the dog going to Swansea. When asked if any other means of destroying the dog had occurred to him he replied, "No, I think drowning is quick and I went in the middle of the night because everything is quiet and peaceful."

The man's defending solicitor then addressed the magistrate saying that it required a degree of courage to destroy a dog that had been a companion, and suggested to the magistrate that his client had not been wanton or unreasonable in carrying out this act. He went on to say, "If you can't pay a vet to destroy a dog, what are you to do, stick a knife in it? My client did the best he could in the circumstances." After hearing all the evidence the magistrate found the man guilty as charged and gave him a fine with costs and a two-year disqualification from keeping a dog. The defence solicitor stated that this was not a flagrant case of cruelty, and that his client would be very upset. My reply to that was "Good!"

CHAPTER 17

El Tambo

The more senior members of the inspectorate had told me that at some point I would deal with an incident that would turn out to be the crowning pinnacle of my career. I had been told that every inspector had that one job that he is remembered for. Little did I know that on Wednesday 9th February 1977 this was going to be that occasion for me. I was listening to the local radio station as I was driving to my next call when a newsflash came over the air: "The fire damaged freighter, *El Tambo*, off the coast of Fishguard in Wales that has over 900 cattle on board, has been boarded by the crew from the Royal Navy survey vessel *H.M.S. Herald.*" The newsreader gave more information about the freighter and told his listening public that the captain of the Sealink's ferry, the *Avalon,* had said that he and his passengers onboard the ferry had a grandstand seat as flames had shot 30ft into the air and enveloped the stern of the *El Tambo*. The lifeboats from the *Avalon* had taken the 21-man crew off the stricken ship and the freighter was now being towed towards Fishguard by a Naval salvage vessel the *Gargarney* operating out the local port of Pembroke Dock.

I stopped my vehicle at the side of the road and tried to take in what I had just heard, trying to figure out what part if any I, as the local inspector for Fishguard, should be doing. What would my gaffers at RSPCA Headquarters be thinking and wanting me to do? Well with my foot firmly down on the accelerator, I headed towards Fishguard not knowing what I would find, or what I would do. Within a very short time I arrived at Fishguard Harbour and was conversing with the local coastguard whom I had met on a previous occasion. He briefed me on the latest report on the *El Tambo*. I asked him about the cattle and he said, "Yes, I thought you might ask about them. There are over 900 of them onboard and they were on their way to Libya. We do not know at this stage how they have been affected by the fire."

After speaking on his land-to-ship radio I was asked if I would like to be taken out to meet the freighter and take a look at the cattle. After a quick telephone call to my headquarters they confirmed that they had heard the news and were being bombarded by calls from news media and members of the public asking what the RSPCA was doing about the cattle. HQ told me that a senior officer had been given the job of coordinating all the information about the freighter. I was to liase directly with him giving him any information I could, as soon as I had it. Having kitted myself out with the necessary lifesaving jacket I found myself on a small coastguard boat, speeding across Fishguard Harbour and heading out to sea. It did not take long before the fritillary of salvage vessels and the cattle freighter came into view.

Onboard *El Tambo* the smell of the dowsed fire was choking and I could see smoke was still pouring out of various escape holes in the engine room and the wheelhouse. I found that the ship had four decks of cattle; the cattle were housed side by side in single stalls along the ship's length. The floor of each deck had several inches of water that had come from the fire hoses putting out the fire. The lower I went into the ship the more water there was on the floor because the water was now flowing from the upper decks down to the lower decks. I found myself in over 2ft of water on the very lowest deck. The water had mixed with the dung and the urine from the animals and the stench and ammonia content was overpowering. There was no ventilation and no lighting, as the electrical supply had been destroyed by the fire. Surprisingly all the cattle that I saw were in sound condition. Some were making a hell of a racket with their bellowing but this was quite understandable under the circumstances. Back on the top deck I spoke with the captain of the *El Tambo* who informed me, much to my horror, that none of the cattle had been fed or watered since yesterday; it was now midday. I was shown a good grade of hay that had not been contaminated by the water or the fire.

The captain of the naval vessel *Gargarney* agreed that he would get his crew to fix up a water supply direct from his vessel, but this would take until the early hours of the next day to set up. In the meantime with the help from the naval crew and some of the crew from *El Tambo* who had returned after abandoning the ship, I was able to give some of the hay to the cattle and by means of buckets supply each animal with a quantity of water. It was very late that evening when I finished that first task and the freighter had now been anchored just outside Fishguard Harbour. The general plan seemed to be that come daybreak everything was going to be sorted and all the animals be removed. I made my report to my officer at Headquarters, telling them my concerns for the animals' welfare and urged that pressure be put on the 'powers that be' to get the cattle off this ship as soon as possible.

El Tambo
Photograph: Courtesy of The Western Telegraph

I left the ship late that evening and returned home. Bright and early the next morning I was again aboard the *El Tambo* but I had a feeling that this day was not going to be good. Men from the Ministry of Agriculture had come aboard, as had various naval officers and other people claiming to have salvage rights on the freighter. They were all in great discussion and heated debate in different parts of the ship. I did not get involved with these matters but along with various members of the crew and one of the Ministry officials, whom I knew quite well as we worked in the local cattle market together, we made an inspection of the cattle. We found none were dead but the ammonia smell and the general conditions had worsened considerably over the past few hours. I returned to the top deck to find out the outcome of these so-called discussions and to see when the animals were going to be removed. I was told that the captain of the *El Tambo* was so upset and outraged by the various claims of salvage rights on his vessel he was now refusing to accept anyone's help, including mine.

One of my colleagues from Swansea arrived to give me a hand and together we spoke on our own to the captain of the *El Tambo*. We were not talking about salvage rights; we were talking about animal welfare rights. After a while the captain agreed that as long as the RSPCA remained on board his ship and supervised the welfare of the cattle, he would allow electricity and the water supply to be connected from the naval vessel *Gargarney*. By now many firms had sent their representatives to the *El Tambo* to argue their case regarding salvage rights. On board there were representatives from Switzerland, Plymouth, London, Milford Haven, Fishguard and Pembroke Dock. In my opinion, and I did express it at the time, the situation was getting out of control and was becoming very political. Later in the day even more representatives arrived from different parts of the globe and due to all this delay the water and electricity had still not been provided. So my colleague and I with help from some of the crew again had the arduous task of hand feeding the 917 cattle on board the freighter. I stayed on board the *Gargarney* that night, as it was very late when I finished. In fact I'm sure I never actually went to sleep I just put my head on a pillow and it seemed that some ship's cook said, "Here you are John, eggs and bacon. It's breakfast time."

71

Back on the *El Tambo* things seemed to be moving with the water line. The electricity supply had been set up and I could now see on every deck but the ammonia was so bad, I had to get the *Gargarney* to use a compressed air machine to pump air into the lower decks so that I could breathe. My concern now was that some of the cattle were looking poorly. They were swaying in their stalls and those that were lying down were in several inches of contaminated water. It was now midday on Friday and water was being pumped on board. The problem was to make sure each cow had their fill but not too much as this would cause them to become blown. This was worse than not having the water in the first place. As yet I had not lost an animal and I was determined I was not going to lose any.

My patience was running low. In my ship-to-shore telephone calls to HQ I continued asking for someone with the authority to get the animals off the freighter, as they had now been on board for over a week. There was growing concern from the general public, who had not seen what I had seen, as no news media had been allowed on board to film it. Local farmers had offered to buy the consignment of cattle valued at over a £250,000 pounds. Friday came and went. I again slept that night on the naval vessel *Gargarney*. Around midday on the Saturday I was making one of my inspections of the lower decks. At this level there was a small service door that opened out at sea level. This door had been closed and I had been told right from the start of this operation that this door should not be opened due to safety reasons. Although air was still being pumped down into the fourth deck where I was, the ammonia content was overpowering.

Regardless of the instructions that had been given and taking the responsibility into my own hands I opened this small service door. The breeze and fresh air that came through that door was unlike anything I had ever witnessed before. Even the cattle immediately adjacent to the door responded to it. As I looked out of the door onto the calm sea of the harbour, I saw a small rowing boat that had a film crew aboard. The reporter had a microphone in his hand and he was talking to another man who was holding a television camera, they were obviously making a television report and trying to capture the scene. I recognised the reporter as one that I had worked with on other RSPCA stories. On finishing his interview he saw me and called out to me. We exchanged a few greetings and general banter. Now I knew that the media had been restrained from getting a full shot of the true conditions on board, some reporters and television crews had even hired helicopters in an attempt to get that one shot that would make a sensational story. I did not wish to upset anyone on the top deck who were engaged in negotiating, but I thought if this film crew just happened to be lucky enough, being in the right place at the right time as Inspector Norman was taking a fresh air break and they just happened to film the interiors and the conditions on the bottom decks, then how could I be blamed?

That night on the *News at Ten* a film was shown of the plight of the cattle on board the stricken freighter *El Tambo*, anchored in Fishguard Harbour. The newsreader stated that the Admiralty Marshall had placed the *El Tambo* under arrest and a writ had been nailed to its mast. The reporter then went on to show the conditions seen earlier that day by the film crew. Later that evening after the *News at Ten* reports, a call was made to the RSPCA on behalf of the Prime Minister Jim Callaghan. After getting confirmation that what he had just seen on the *News at Ten* was a true definition of the conditions the cattle and I were enduring he, the Prime Minister, ordered his junior Agricultural Minister to be despatched to Fishguard to cut through the red tape and get the animals off the freighter.

On Sunday morning the junior minister arrived by helicopter. After talking briefly to the captain of the naval vessel *Gargarney*, he came over to me and he shook my hand and started to inform me of his intentions. He told me that two vessels were on their way from Holland. These vessels were purposely-built animal transport carriers. One was named the *Hereford Express* and the other the *Normand Express*, a rather appropriate name I thought. With that the junior minister went off with other officials to make small talk about whatever these people make small talk about. I was by now in full conversation with various engineers and maintenance men from the *Gargarney*. It was decided to construct a ramp at the dockside that would allow the cattle to be transferred from the *El Tambo* onto the Dutch ships when they arrived.

After the junior minister left in his helicopter, it was like a beehive of activity: boats, men, timber, chains, hay and water. We did not stop until late afternoon. The captain of the *Normand Express* asked if I would board his ship and inspect its contents. I can assure you the comparison between the *El Tambo* and this ship was like a doss house to a five-star hotel. We all worked through the night till every animal had been transferred off the *El Tambo* and onto the two Dutch ships. One by one they went; I felt like Noah. We finished late on Monday afternoon and I watched as the two Dutch ships sailed out of the harbour on their way to Libya, all 917 cattle safely on board. I had not lost one. I left Fishguard around 4.30p.m. on that Monday afternoon. It was only when I stopped and looked back down to the harbour, and I saw the now empty *El Tambo* that I realised what a job of work had been done. Once again I felt so proud to be an RSPCA Inspector.

There had been many news reports and newspaper stories regarding the incident with the *El Tambo* over the last few days. I received many citations from members of the public including a telegram from the Irish Prime Minister, one from the Animal Sanctuary of Ireland and another from the Faculty of Veterinary Medicine at the University of Tripoli. It was this department that had inspected the cattle on arrival in Libya, the original destination port before the fire. I had received other letters of appreciation; one was from Mr Jim Callaghan the Prime Minister and one from the junior minister who had visited the *El Tambo*. Both letters stated to the Society that they were very impressed with my efforts and dedication, my outstanding service and devotion to duty, which over a number of days had helped to safeguard the welfare of the cattle. These comments and those from the general public, made me eternally grateful for their support and appreciation.

On top of all this the council of the RSPCA awarded me The Elsie M.J. Evans Award. It was the first time this award had been presented to an inspector. A Mr Evans had bequeathed this award in 1975 in memory of his wife. He had requested that such an award be given for an act of bravery or outstanding kindness to animals along with a legacy of £200. This sum of money had been invested in a fund and had accrued interest.

Yes, I hear you ask, what became of the *El Tambo*? Well on Sunday, 27th March 1977 it sank suddenly and mysteriously in Fishguard Harbour. A witness said the stricken freighter gave no warning that she was about to sink. The harbourmaster watched as she suddenly keeled over completely on her side and started to sink. He had stated, "Half an hour earlier she seemed alright; it was all over in ten minutes." Another witness who saw the *El Tambo* sink, said that the bow went down first and then the stern came up, and down she went.

Efforts were being made to unravel the massive legal tangle that now surrounded the sunken cattle freighter. Once again legal battles were taking place regarding who should have the salvage rights of the wreck. The Department of the Environment felt she could have become their own personal nightmare that they might have had to leave her to rot forever and that she would act as a mini breakwater in Fishguard Harbour.

El Tambo
Photograph: Courtesy of The Western Telegraph

CHAPTER 18

Where to now?

After the events of the previous few months especially with the high profile publicity of the *El Tambo* I was on cloud nine, but all this was about to change. The Society had decided that there was going to be a change in our contracts as regards to being transferred every seven years. There had been some financial difficulties within the Society and we had managed to pull through without sacrificing our aims in animal welfare, but it had caused the Society's ruling body to reconsider the whole matter of moving the Inspectorate around. An order had been issued to all staff outlining the intentions of the RSPCA Council on this matter. We were told that in the future when a station became vacant, instead of the old way whereby a superintendent at HQ would choose which inspector would be moved to fill the post, the new method would be that the station would be advertised within the inspectorate. Any inspector who had served at least five years and wanted to be considered for that vacancy could apply for an interview. All candidates would be interviewed and the Society's management would then choose one of those inspectors to be transferred.

It also meant that if an inspector was in a station and had at least one transfer in his career and his present station suited him then he and his family could put down strong roots and forge a strong relationship with that area. I had been in Haverfordwest now for some five years and my family and I had been well accepted by the wonderful Welsh people. We had made friends with some of the nicest people anyone could hope to meet. But despite this and despite the magnificent coastline of Pembrokeshire, its rolling hills and valleys Sandra and I were spending hours pondering over what was going to be the best possible future for Peter and Sara. As lovely as the area was, the job prospects for the kids in ten or twelve years time had to be taken into account and I had this nagging in my bones that out there, there was more for me to do too.

I was an animal advocate that had waged war on cruelty and I felt I should be going to fresh battlefields. So we made up our minds that I would put in for a transfer before the new ruling came into force and we would leave it to someone else to decide where in England or Wales we would next pitch our tent.

CHAPTER 19

Dorset here I come

Well my request to leave Wales had not gone down too well with some of the branch members in Haverfordwest but I had been told that their disappointment was strictly a selfish one, as they did not want another branch to have my services. These remarks made it easier for Sandra and I to accept our decision to move on. It was nice to know that in the short time we had been in Wales they wanted us to stay but they were wishing us well for the future.

I had received a telephone call from Chief Inspector John Dunn stationed at Salisbury. "Morning Inspector," he said, "I understand you are coming to Blandford." "Bradford?" I said. "No," said the Chief, "Blandford Forum, it's in Dorset." "What makes you think that?" I asked him. "I have had an instruction from HQ this morning, telling me that Inspector Norman will shortly be transferred from his present station in Haverfordwest to take up his duties in the vacant station at Blandford Forum," he replied. "Well that all sounds pretty clear," I said, "pity nobody told me." "You know what they are like in Headquarters," he said, "never letting your left hand know what your right hand is doing!" "Anyway, I will be your new Chief and I just wanted you to know that if you and your good lady wanted to have a quick visit before you move, let me know and I will arrange for you to have a key to the property in Blandford," he said.

I told Sandra and like me she was at a loss as to where Blandford was. So, as before, we went out and purchased maps and guidebooks. Once again I was amazed at the area; again I would have some beautiful coastline, from Lulworth Cove almost to Bournemouth Pier. It was a large branch stretching up into the Dorset countryside past Shaftesbury into Gillingham and across the land to Cranborne Chase, Alderholt and down into the picturesque villages that ran back towards Bournemouth. It took a few days after the Chief's telephone call for my instruction to arrive and it was confirmed that on Monday, 11th April 1977 the Normans would invade Dorset.

As before the family had to be settled into their new home. Peter had to find new friends in his new school but like most kids he seemed to take all this upheaval in his stride. Sara only being four was very adaptable, and Sandra, well those who know Sandra know how she copes with it all, the same way she copes with everything that is put in her way. She just copes, she just does it, she doesn't ask why me, or say why should I, she just does it. She has always been the kingpin in my career. I am paid to do the job; she, as you have read earlier, became the unpaid member of staff.

I know what she has to put up with. You ask yourself this: how would you feel when your favourite TV show is switched off while your RSPCA husband takes a telephone call or sees to a caller at the door who wishes to bring to his attention the plight of an animal? Or perhaps be woken at 2.00am by the bedside phone calling out your RSPCA husband to alleviate some suffering of an animal? Or how about breaking off halfway through a barney with your RSPCA husband while he takes yet another telephone call from some member of the public? Well I'll tell you what Sandra does, she does all of these things time and time again. She misses Coronation Street, she lies awake after he has been called out at night and waits for his safe return and with regards to the unfinished barney she will patiently wait in the kitchen for the second round. All my work is nothing without the little woman and here she was again helping me to settle into Dorset, and running around after two young kids, and doing what Sandra does best, coping.

The Blandford branch was turning out to be all right. I had made my first visit to my new branch secretary, a Mr Tom Dean, and what a gent he was, ex-military, just the sort of man I could communicate with, straight down the middle talking, no ifs no buts. I had the feeling that Tom and I would get along just fine. I wished I could have said the same for the superintendent of the police I went to see at Blandford Police Station. Blimey, I thought I was a straight talker but this man took the biscuit. I had called in at the police station to introduce myself as the new inspector for the area and in order to break the ice I took with me an instruction that I had received that morning from HQ informing the entire inspectorate that a new arrangement had been agreed by the RSPCA and all chief constables. As from the date stated on this instruction the police would now be responsible for cats that are injured on the road. Up to this date the police only had a responsibility for dogs injured on the highway.

The instruction asked all inspectors to make a visit to their local police stations bringing this new agreement to the notice of the senior officer, in case he or she had not received it from their superiors. Armed with a smile and this piece of news I visited the local police station. The desk sergeant shook my hand; he read the instruction and shook his head even harder. "So Inspector," he said, "you wish to show this to my superintendent do you?" "Yes please, Sarge," I said, still wearing my best smile. "This way then," said the sergeant shrugging his shoulders and giving out a big sigh. We walked down a corridor to an office not far from the main door. It turned out that I would be quite pleased it was so close to the main door. "Yes?" said a voice inside the office after the sergeant had knocked just the once. The sergeant went inside the office, leaving me outside the closed door.

Within a few seconds the door opened wide. A stocky man wearing a superintendent's insignia on his uniform looked at me. "Sir," I said, "I'm Inspector Norman…" I did not get the RSPCA bit out. The superintendent put his arm around my shoulder but not in a friendly manner as I thought he was going to do. He turned me around and by holding my collar at the back of my neck he frogmarched me towards the main door. The sergeant said nothing; he just walked ahead of us and opened the large swing door at the entrance to the station. I was half lifted and half placed outside the station. The superintendent said, "I have had enough of the RSPCA over the years. I don't want you or

81

anyone else from your Society telling me what I am responsible for!" With that the door closed. I told you that I was grateful that his office was close to the main door. I stood there a little while expecting Jeremy Beadle to jump out, but he never did! I could see the sergeant now back behind his desk. His eyes met mine and he just shook his head very slowly. I could imagine what he was saying: "Well you said you wanted to show that piece of paper to my superintendent!"

I arrived home and told Sandra about my visit to the police station. "Was it alright?" she said. "Yes, great reception," I said, "I think it must be a tradition down here in Dorset to make you feel welcome, funny tradition really." I then went on to explain what had taken place earlier at the station. "I don't believe it," Sandra said, "you must have misunderstood". "Yes," I said, "I must have, the fact that only one of my feet touched the floor from the office to the main door, must have been me misunderstanding something." I had not been in the house more than a few minutes when Sandra informed me that a police officer was walking up the driveway. I looked and saw my friendly neighbourhood police superintendent knocking on my front door. I was going to shout, "Yes?" but thought better of it. Instead I did the next best thing - I opened the door. The superintendent stuck out his right hand, grabbed my right hand and shook it harder than the sergeant had shaken his head. "Sorry, Inspector," he said, "my fault; you are right." He was waving the instruction in his left hand; I had forgotten I had left it with him. "You see," he said, "over the years we have had very little cooperation from the RSPCA and you walking into my station with this piece of paper was the last straw. Anyway I have made my enquiries and you are quite right to bring it to my attention. Now Inspector if there is anything you want, anything I or my officers can do to help you just call at the station and we will see what we can do."

I was still being shook by the hand as I said, "Thank you, Sir." The superintendent then let me go and went off as swiftly as he had arrived, my hand still vibrating from his handshake. Sandra came to the door and said, "Was that him?" "Yes," I said, "and he will do for me." I added, "Anybody in his position who can accept being wrong and can come and apologise in that way is a man I can get on with." My other visits to the police stations in the area were all a little easier but they all were very wary of making me feel at home. I had the same sort of edgy response at the vets as well. I would pull up in their car park, see one or more of the vets through the windows yet by the time I went into the surgery the receptionist was telling me that all the vets were out or very busy.

Over several weeks I turned this cold reception around at all the police stations and vets. My main spiel to them was "If I am a **** then I am a **** but don't call me one just because someone else was one!" This attitude and my enthusiasm for the work soon found me walking into these establishments and putting the kettle on. Now when you can do that you know you have been accepted.

CHAPTER 20

Back to Wales

No, I had not been kicked out of Dorset but after spending a very short time at Blandford Forum there had been an oil pollution disaster. An oil tanker *Eleni V* had gone aground and spilled thousands and thousands of tons of crude oil into the sea off the shore at Pembrokeshire. HQ had sent me back to Haverfordwest to help in the cleaning up operation. I knew the area, had many contacts and by working alongside the present inspector and others who had been drafted into Pembrokeshire we commenced the long and time-consuming task of collecting the oiled sea birds that were in their hundreds along the coast. We had to decide by assessing the condition the birds were in at the time whether they had a chance of survival or whether P.T.S was the kindest option. Unfortunately it was the latter in many of the cases.

Many oiled birds being collected were gannets. These magnificent birds were a sorry sight with black crude oil now covering their once brilliant white feathers. The birds that we thought did stand a chance of survival had to be boxed and then transported to our oil pollution cleaning centre in Taunton. It was a long road journey, and the stress of being handled, boxed and transported for several hours was taking its toll on the birds. I visited my old contacts at the RAF base in Brawdy just outside Haverfordwest and met up with a captain I had known whilst in the area and to my great joy he arranged through his commanding officers to fly all the boxed birds to their base in Yeovil just a few miles away from our centre in Taunton.

Over the next few weeks the RAF flew hundreds of the oiled birds in their Wessex helicopters and their generosity saved many of the birds' lives. Over the weeks and months we released back into the sea fully fit and clean birds. I also had the pleasure of flying with the birds in the helicopters. Who said this job doesn't have any perks?

The Flight of the Gannets
Photograph: Courtesy of The Western Telegraph

CHAPTER 21

Bambi

On Thursday, 25th May 1978 a roe deer stag was born. Its entry into the world would touch the hearts of all who heard its story. It was on that day that two forestry workers in the Cranborne area came across the body of an adult female roe deer. She had a massive wound just below the neck; it was a wound that these forestry workers had seen before. After a search it was later confirmed that piano wire had been stretched between two trees and poachers had chased the female deer causing her to injure herself as she slammed into the wire trap. From where the wire was found it seems the deer managed to keep going with her injuries until she dropped with exhaustion. The shock of what had happened had brought on the birth. The fawn was only hours old and it was lying at the side of his mother's dead body. It was obvious to the finders that in the dying moments of the deer's life she had bitten through the umbilical cord and then licked her son clean before she died.

The fawn arrived at my house within half an hour of it being found and its outsized fluttering eyelashes gave no hint of man's cruelty that had caused our meeting. Sandra had already started to prepare for its arrival by getting out the baby orphan feeding equipment. This was a box of tricks that I had collected over the years. It contained syringes and various baby feeders and lots of different foods that could be prepared for various species of animals. Milk was the main item on the deer's menu and by Sandra concocting a mixture of cows' milk, babies' milk and glucose it was not long before the deer was filling its belly for the first time. Sara called him Bambi saying, "I love him, he is so gentle and sweet. He is just like the little deer on the cartoon."

After a short feed I took Bambi to the local vet for a check up. He said that the deer faced a danger as he lacked colostrums that he would have got from his mother's milk. Over the next few days everything went well and then Bambi began to develop problems just as the vet had predicted. The chance of survival was very slim and every hour the deer was getting weaker. The vet injected massive amounts of drugs and vitamins but with the deer not taking food he would die. Sandra tried every concoction and variation she knew but each bottle that she mixed was rejected. The scene reminded me of the one in the film *Born Free* when Virginia McKenna, who was portraying the part of the woman trying to hand rear Elsa the lioness, made each bottle of milk with a different concoction. The lioness rejected its milk and, like Bambi, it seemed to be slipping away and losing the battle.

Peter, Sara and Bambi

Sandra then mixed up some baby powder and added glucose with a spoonful of condensed milk and various powdered vitamins. As she offered this to the deer I heard her say, "Yes, it's going down. He's drinking it." After daily trips to the vets for injections, Bambi went from strength to strength and overcame this initial scare. Many 'so called experts' had contacted me over the previous few days telling me that what I was trying to do had been tried on many occasions and everyone had failed and so would I. Well here was that failure of a deer in my garden with my two children Peter and Sara. He was eating my roses and playing hide and seek in the long grass.

Now what do you do with a 14-week-old deer that has become domesticated? This is not something as an RSPCA inspector I would have recommended anyone to do. All wild animals coming into the Society's care must have a chance of survival in the wild after their treatment. The Society does not want them to go into a sanctuary or be enclosed for the rest of their lives, but to be released back into the wild from where they came. I had made that decision to give Bambi his life back weeks ago and had made contact with a man who lived out in the wilds of Dorset. He was a schoolteacher at a very large private school and he had a cottage in the grounds that backed onto open fields and woodland where deer were known to be living. As a bonus to all this, he had at the side of his cottage a double tennis court that had not been used as such for many years. The fencing was still intact but the inside of the courts was completely overgrown with vegetation. Could this have been any more ideal?

I could not believe my luck and on meeting the schoolteacher in those early days of Bambi's life we had a plan of action and we were waiting for that day when the deer would be fit and well and ready to be released back into the wild. That day came about two weeks later.

The first stage was to put Bambi in the enclosure and feed him on a concentration of nuts and other foods that he had taken with great gusto over several weeks. This mixture provided a balanced diet that captive deer feed on. The idea was to gradually spread the food about the court making Bambi go and find it as opposed to being fed from a container.

The second stage was to give him less and less human contact. Food was thrown over the fence and the teacher kept well away from making any visual or vocal contact with him.

All went well and one morning the teacher was looking out of his bedroom window when he saw two wild deer that had come out of the woods and were standing at the fence of the old tennis court next to Bambi. All three of them were sniffing at each other through the fence. We decided that night that the gate on the fence would be left open just to see what would happen.

Well we did this for three nights and Bambi made no attempt to leave the fenced area. We knew he had found the open gate as we had put some of his food outside the fence. That went, but not Bambi. We did not know what to do for the best, but he gave us the answer. On the fourth morning of leaving the gate open the teacher phoned me "He's gone," he said, "nowhere to be seen." I did not know what to say really. Was I glad or not? Anyway I went to the cottage and did a complete search of every inch of the tennis court and sure enough, Bambi had gone.

I stayed all day at the cottage peering through the binoculars at the woods a few hundred yards away. If I could see Bambi just one more time I thought, that would satisfy my curiosity that he was alright. I would easily recognise him as he had a large white patch on his side that had been there since day one. It was as though three or four of the white fawn spots had all merged together leaving one big spot. The next day, nothing although some deer had been seen at the edge of the woods feeding in the field that ran up the slope to the woods. On the third day I took Peter and Sara with me to the cottage. I had this idea that if I got Sara to sit in the field near the woods and call his name as she had done countless times over the past weeks it might be possible that Bambi would hear her and respond to her voice. What a silly idea I told myself but it was an idea I wanted to try.

Sara sat in the field for ages calling out in a way only children can. "Bambi, Bambi," time and time again, "Bambi, Bambi," she cried. Her voice was getting as low as my depression, and then I saw several deer at the edge of the woods. Two or three of them came into the field. I was behind a hedge with Peter and the teacher and I told Sara to call out very softly. "Bambi, Bambi," she said. I could see the deer looking about themselves and as they heard Sara's voice they all bounced back into the woods, all but one deer. It stood there with its nostrils twitching. It seemed to be taking in the sound of her voice.

He started to walk a few steps away from the edge of the woods. I whispered out to Sara to call Bambi again. She did and this time like a dog returning to its master it scampered, leapt and bounded towards Sara. I could see the tears in her eyes. "Bambi, Bambi, hello," she said as he sniffed and nudged at her tiny body. The three of us behind the hedge did not make a move; we just looked taking in this unlikely event as it developed.

Peter stared; I cried. No I didn't; the teacher cried, he smiled and he stared. Bambi allowed Sara to touch him but within a few minutes he scampered back off up the hill towards the woods leaving Sara standing there and shouting "Bambi" after him. I went over to her just as he was disappearing into the woods and explained to Sara that we had done all that we could have done for Bambi and that he would be all right.

I returned several times to the cottage. I saw several deer in the field but hand on heart I never could say I saw Bambi again. The teacher did on many occasions over the months. He recognised him by the white spot. Bambi was with all the other deer and as soon as the teacher made himself known in the field, all of the deer including the now wild Bambi disappeared into their safe haven.

CHAPTER 22

Make my day

These are little stories that have really made my day, the kind of incidents that keep RSPCA inspectors going. When we are coping with some of the most unscrupulous people you can imagine, to deal with more pleasant human beings is a real tonic. What could be more of a tonic than Violet, a grand lady of 86. A social worker told me that Violet kept a canary in a cage and the domestic helper had reported back to the social services that they thought the bird had died. They did not like to tell Violet as she thought it was all right and that the bird had been sitting on the bottom of the cage just resting. I visited Violet and saw that her beloved pet canary named "Angel" was now just that, and had been one for several days. I explained the best way I could to this darling of a lady. "How will I ever replace my Angel?" she asked, her tears matching my own. "I think I know where I can find another one just like Angel," I said. "I shall be back before long." I took Angel and the old tattered cage with me and I returned to my home.

Little did Violet know that she had picked on the only RSPCA inspector in the south of England who kept canaries. I had a very large aviary on my back garden, which contained various species of birds: foreign finches, canaries and some wild birds recovering from injuries. I spent many an hour in my aviary tackling the world's problems, going through scenarios that were part of my daily life and then when I came out of my aviary I felt that yet again I could tackle the world. I chose a canary that was a very close likeness to Angel. Then I called on Steve Fowler, the proprietor of one of the biggest chains of pet shops in the area. I have known Steve for many years and I told him about Violet. Steve understood why I was relating this story to him and without me asking he donated a very large cage for Violet's new bird. Also being the kind of man he is, Steve arranged that Violet would have all the seed needed, delivered on a regular basis, free of charge. What a man! I returned to Violet with the donated cage and my donation of a new canary. "Angel," she said when she saw it. "It's my Angel."

RSPCA Inspector John Norman hands over Angel to Violet
Photograph: With kind permission of Daily Echo Bournemouth

The enthusiasm of young children has always got to me. If I am asked to become involved with some visit to spread the gospel according to Inspector Norman: Thou shalt not be cruel to animals, I am always amazed at the interest that these kids show in what I was telling them. You had their attention right from the start. They would stare straight back at you. They would digest every word you were saying and afterwards they always wanted to raise money or get involved in helping the RSPCA in anyway possible. Cranborne Middle School based one of their morning assemblies on animal welfare and I went along to enlighten them on the work of the RSPCA animal shelters that care for unwanted animals. One week later I returned to the school and I filled my van with tins of food collected by the children from the good people in the village of Cranborne. You expect a few tins but on this occasion I was met with a mountain of tins.

Pupils at Cranborne Middle School
Photograph: With kind permission of the Daily Echo Bournemouth

There were three young girls in Bournemouth. After one of their friends had lost their hamster they decided in its memory they would do a sponsored walk between the two piers of Boscombe and Bournemouth. They were sponsored to the tune of £152.00, which they donated to the RSPCA.

The girls on their sponsored walk between the two piers
Photograph: With kind permission of the Daily Echo Bournemouth

The same type of response came from the Hampreston First School with stacks and stacks of food donated by the children.

Pupils of
Hampreston C of E School
with
John Norman
Photograph:
With kind permission
of the Daily Echo Bournemouth

John Norman with members of Corfe Mullen Guides
Photograph: With kind permission of the Daily Echo Bournemouth

There was a group of girl guides in Corfe Mullen who staged a 'stay awake' and a fashion show in support of the RSPCA. They raised £460.00.

It's not only children; adults at times come out with some real concern for animal welfare in areas that you don't expect. There was a firm of developers in the Poole area that had got the job of clearing a large piece of land in preparation for the building of a new factory and a recreation area. On the land was a large high sandy bank that was being used by sand martins for nesting. I brought this to the attention of the firm's directors and without argument they held up the production of this site for several weeks at great expense to themselves. They rescheduled some of their work and they managed to give the birds the chance to finish their nesting. Yes, it's these kind of acts that keep an inspector going.

CHAPTER 23

Grapes

You can bet your bottom dollar that if I got a call from the police asking for advice it was something to do with an animal and members of the public; a situation they were powerless to resolve but that a RSPCA inspector could sort out. Such a call came from the local police on 10th September 1980. "John," I heard a voice I recognised say down the phone, "John can you call in and see me as soon as possible?" he asked. "Does that mean right now, Sarge?" I said. "Your powers of observation are first class, Inspector," he replied. I had known this police officer for several years and we always exchanged this type of verbal banter. Within the hour I was drinking his coffee as he was enlightening me of the problem. "We had a telephone call from one of the shopkeepers in town telling us that two women were walking about town carrying what looked like a large dog in a blanket." "Yes, so," I said, "what's the problem?" "The shop man stated that he asked the women if the dog was alright. The eldest of these two women said that everything was alright but the man has said that the dog was stinking to high heaven," said the sergeant. "How long ago was this?" I asked. "Just before I rang you," he replied. "I sent one of the lads round and he is with the females now at the other end of town. He reported back that the dog is ill, very ill, but that the two females are very reluctant to speak to him."

As my presence in the crowded shopping area would only alienate them even further I said, "Get your constable to tell them I am at the police station and I would like to see their dog, just to make sure it's alright and tell them if the dog needs veterinary treatment then the RSPCA could help out." The sergeant made radio contact with his colleague and after a few 'ifs and buts' we were told that the two women had agreed to accompany the officer to the police station but they were not happy. The two women, who were in fact mother and daughter, arrived and they were escorted into the station by way of the back door. One

96

was holding a tartan travelling rug up close to her face. I could see the features of a dog's legs hanging out from the bottom of the rug and what could be a dog's muzzle pressed up close under the carrier's chin.

I tried to be as polite as I could, and I really can be polite when I try, but these women were having none of it. "You're not putting it to sleep," said the eldest of the women. "Nobody has said anything about putting the dog to sleep," I replied, "but can I have a look at it?" The woman cuddled the bundle even closer to herself. "It's alright," said the younger woman. "It doesn't smell too healthy to me," chirped one of the passing constables. That was just the sort of comment I wanted at this stage. I asked the woman to put the dog down on the floor so that she could show me what the problem was and I could see if I could be of any assistance to them. My polite mode was obviously working as the dog was carefully laid on the floor. As I gently unwrapped the rug from around the dog it continued to lie there as, in my opinion, it was dying. There was no weight on it and it was completely emaciated. The last time I had seen a dog as thin as this it was a dead dog. How it was staying alive I do not know. It did not move; in fact the only sign of life came from an irregular breathing pattern and the gentle sorrowful blink of an eye.

The two women were now both crying and stroking the dog. "Why is it so thin?" I asked in a voice that conveyed my utter disbelief in what I was looking at. "We feed the dog on grapes. We are vegans, we don't feed our animals on meat," said one of the women. I knew without any doubt that, regardless of the reason given, the dog was not being provided with proper care and attention and that no vet would allow a dog in this bodily condition to be kept alive. The women refused to allow me to take the dog to a vet so I gave them both a caution. Having found that it would take too long for a vet to attend the police station I asked them if they would sign the dog over to the RSPCA so that I could do what I felt was necessary. Both women flatly refused this request so after consulting with the sergeant I took it upon myself, accepting full responsibility for my actions, to put the dog to sleep.

97

The women called me all the names under sun and told me that I would be hearing from their solicitors. Later a vet examined the dog, which was a rough collie (like Lassie), and he provided a statement that the dog had been caused unnecessary suffering and the act of putting it to sleep was warranted and justified in the interests of the dog.

I saw their solicitor some weeks later in the local magistrates court as he represented his clients on a plea of guilty to causing the unnecessary suffering of the dog. As one of the women was returning to her seat after giving evidence she attacked me hitting me with her handbag and shouting "Murderer". Both women were found guilty. They were each given a fine and both given a three-year ban on keeping dogs. When you look at the photograph of this dog remember that seconds before this photograph was taken the dog was alive!

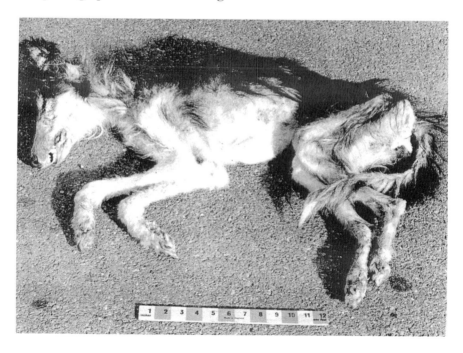

Photograph of the emaciated dog

98

CHAPTER 24

50

27th May 1995 my 50th birthday. It was going to be a very good day as a few months ago Sara and her fiancé Paul stated that they would like to be married on my 50th birthday. Well what can one say? It was going to be a day to remember for everyone. Sara had asked that our relations from far and wide be invited, most of them live in Mansfield, so I made arrangements for the reception to be held at a local motel restaurant that was owned by a very good friend of mine. These wonderful people put on a first class wedding reception. They also gave me a very good rate for the many rooms that were needed to accommodate all of our guests; it really was a great day. I knew a man who attended all the local and county agricultural shows in his old brewery wagon pulled by two big, black, shire horses. Mr Beck, the owner of this team, put on a fabulous spectacle and he agreed to take Sara and I to the church on this splendid wagon pulled by these magnificent shire horses. After the service Sara and Paul would be taken to the motel by Mr Beck and his team. It really was a wonderful sight. Motorists stopped their cars and got out and many people watched from the pavement and applauded as we rode by.

Like all parents at one of their children's weddings you wonder what the future will hold for the newlyweds. Sara and Paul were well matched and I know one of Sara's greatest wishes was for her to have a family. She had always doted on any baby or young child that had entered our lives. So a few years into their marriage it was no surprise to be told that we were going to be grandparents. For Sandra and I this was going to be yet another of our ambitions fulfilled. When you are raising a family it only seems that other people's children get married and turn them into grandparents but now it was going to be our turn and we could not wait.

After a few months into the pregnancy Paul phoned to say that Sara was in hospital and it looked like she was going to lose the baby and she was asking for me to visit her. I was at the hospital within minutes. I was there to solve the problem. Like most dads we think we can solve all problems for our kids. I had it all worked out in my head as I drove to the hospital; I would tell Sara not to worry and that there would be other times when everything would be fine. I was shown Sara's bed and went through the curtains. There I saw not my grown up daughter but my little girl. She was crying and sobbing; she was asking her dad to make things right as he had done all her life, but here I was helpless. I had my little girl holding me around my neck crying and telling me she was so sorry. Those words creased me. My head and body were numb. I was told that Sara's baby had died but that Sara was going to have to give birth and this would take some time.

I spoke with Sara saying her all the words that were in my head but as I heard them come out they made no sense. The only thing that I could think of was that this dad had failed to help his daughter; he who had always promised to heal her wounds and take away any pain could only turn away and leave his child to her own ordeal. That day haunted me for months. It was sometime later Sara and Paul planted a pink flowering shrub in their garden in memory as they said to their "little lump". We all stood in the garden on that day. Paul's mum and dad were magnificent in their support. Like all bad stories this one was going to end happily as Sara was expecting again and my joy was only tainted by the sad end to her last pregnancy.

Again all was going well then the phone rang. How is it that you know before you even pick up the receiver that the news is not going to be good? It was Paul saying that Sara was in hospital and had miscarried. I could not believe what I was being told. It seemed once again the man who's job it was to look after her and protect her had failed her.

There was a black cloud over all our heads for months afterwards. Some time later Sara and Paul informed us that their GP, Dr Baker, had carried out some tests on Sara and discovered that she had a rare blood disorder called 'anti-cardio lipid syndrome with phospholipid antibodies' which made her blood clot in the placenta and caused her to miscarry. After Dr Baker did some research on their behalf he discovered that there was hope in that Professor Reagan at St Mary's Hospital in Paddington, London, had been researching into this disorder. She had found that a strict regime of daily intakes of low dose aspirin combined with twice daily self-administered injections of heparin into the stomach, from the day the pregnancy was confirmed, together with extremely close and careful monitoring these women could carry a pregnancy to full term. There were only nine other girls that were known of at the time to have this syndrome but with the medical regime described they had all gone on to have successful pregnancies and live births.

Sara was told that all treatment would be stopped six weeks before the baby was due to be born and that the injections of heparin would be extremely painful but Sara being Sara had agreed with Paul's blessing to try again for a baby, and that Paul would be the one to give the heparin injections to Sara. Some time down the line yet again we were told that we might be grandparents. I smiled and I laughed and I went down to the bottom of the garden and I shouted, "Yes!" but I just had to keep everything under control. As the weeks turned into months everything was just fine and on the 14th October 1998 I became a granddad to Olivia Alice Corfield. Sara and the baby were doing well.

Now my good contacts on the local newspaper had been following Sara's story and were ready to do a feature on the birth informing their readers that Sara was one of only ten girls in the country with this rare syndrome. The storyline was going to be an encouragement to any reader who may have had the misfortune of miscarrying to keep trying as miracles do happen. The photographer from the local paper went to see Sara and Paul to get that happy family shot showing them holding Olivia who was then just nine days old. While the photographs were being taken it seemed that Sara was not responding in her usual manner. She seemed to be very vague and did not seem to understand why the photographer was taking the pictures. Paul was very concerned and he asked Sara if she would like to visit the doctor. Now despite all her medical problems Sara would not voluntarily go to see a doctor unless it was absolutely necessary, but as soon as Paul asked her she put Olivia into his arms and went and sat in the family car.

Paul took Sara and Olivia straight to see the doctor. Unfortunately Dr Baker had gone off duty so one of the other doctors from the practice examined Sara and as a result feared Sara had contracted meningitis. The doctor ordered Paul to rush Sara straight to hospital and gave him a letter to take with him explaining his fears. On arriving at Poole General Hospital Sara's condition had worsened and she was having difficulty giving any information about herself or her new baby. Sara started to have fits so they gave her an emergency MRI brain scan, the results of which required Sara to be rushed by ambulance to the Neurological Department of Southampton General Hospital.

Paul phoned and I took the call. I could not take it in; Sara in hospital, very ill, come quick. Within the hour, and what an hour, Sandra and I stood at the bedside of our little girl. Her eyes were wide open but there was no expression, no movement. We were told that Sara had two blood clots on her brain and that she was now in a coma. If any reader has had a similar experience then they and only they know what we were going through. Paul and Sara, two young people, their only wish in life to enjoy their days as man and wife to raise a family. They had already lost two babies. They had come through it, just nine days ago. Olivia had been born and everything was just perfect but now Sara was in a coma. I could not feel my body and I could not hear anything. All the voices that spoke were in a language that my brain did not or could not understand.

Day after day I watched Sara. I waited as dedicated medical teams did what medical teams do, waited whilst those wonderful human beings we call nurses cleaned and tidied my daughter. They brushed her hair and re-set the many tubes that were attached to her. My son Peter had travelled down from Mansfield to be with his sister. He had brought with him the love from all our friends and relations in and around the Mansfield area but we, that's Sandra, Paul, Paul's mum and dad and me, we could not tell anyone why this was happening or how it would all end. One day a consultant who had been attending Sara and had to the best of his ability tried to give us words of comfort and support asked Paul, Sandra and me to come into his office. He gave us news that day that rocked our lives. He stated that although it's impossible to say how Sara would react to her illness we would have to prepare ourselves to live with what we were seeing now: a girl that would probably never recognise us as parents or never be able to care for Olivia.

How Paul took that news I will never know to my dying day. I know like me the words had gone right through to his bones. Paul could not, Paul would not and Paul never did accept that diagnosis. He looked after his new charge all by himself. He would not let anyone anywhere near Olivia; there was no danger of him being separated from her for even a few moments. Paul videoed hours of Olivia and on seeing those videos you could hear Paul behind the camera talking to Olivia telling her that they were going to the hospital that day to see mummy and that everything would be alright and that when mummy woke up she would see what a beautiful baby she had. On seeing those videos I can only try and explain how I felt. I just wanted my little girl back; what had she done? Why her?

I was standing by the side of Sara's bed one day. In fact it was the first time in nearly two weeks that I had been there on my own. Paul and Sandra were in the family room seeing to Olivia and talking to Peter our son. There I was looking down at Sara. The nurses had made a great job of brushing her hair, a job that I had done thousands of times when she was a young girl. I had always had a habit of touching a baby's nose with my finger and making a noise like a car's horn, "Beep, beep," I would say. Sandra had shouted at me many times for doing this but I had done it to practically every baby that I saw. As I stood there on my own that day I felt I had no more tears to give her; my throat hurt, the muscles in my neck had seized up days ago in my attempt to hold back my grief as I gave friends and family a daily update. I looked at Sara, held out my hand and with my finger I touched the end of Sara's nose "Beep, beep," I said. I could not see her face for my tears, "Beep, beep Sara," I repeated. As I have just said I could not clearly see Sara's face but I saw her hand move and it moved towards my face. She touched my nose with her outstretched finger. She did all this and never moved her head, her body or her eyes. I wanted to shout for help but I could not, dare not take my eyes from her. "Do that again Sara," I said and like the first time she repeated her quest.

I could hear Sandra's voice as she had just witnessed Sara's arm moving from my face and she was asking what was happening. "She touched my nose," I told her. By now Paul and Peter, who was holding Olivia, and two nurses had all joined me around the bed. This was going to be my big day. Dad was going to show the world that he could get Sara to respond from her coma. "Sara," I said, "touch Daddy's nose." I waited – nothing. I repeated my request, nothing. I stared into Sara's face. I wanted to hit her she had let me down. All she had to do was touch my nose. She had just done it. She had done it twice why wouldn't she do it again? I could hear feet shuffling from the other people around the bed; I knew what they were all thinking that it never happened. I knew down the line Peter was holding Olivia. Without turning my eyes from Sara I indicated to Peter that I wanted the baby and I held out my arms in his direction and still my gaze never left Sara. I was too afraid to do so, afraid that she would move and I would miss it. I heard a nurse saying that it would not be a good idea to put the baby so close to Sara at this stage. Once again I made my request that the baby be passed to me and again I heard that authoritative voice of the nurse advising me not to hold the baby close to Sara. "Pass me the bloody baby," I said. I was now using the voice that my family had grown used to and recognised. It was a voice that most people who find themselves in my position use when we are afraid or frightened. We think we are the only ones who can see the light at the end of the tunnel and no one was going to switch it off.

104

"Give him the baby," I heard Peter say. I felt Olivia being put into my arms. I held that precious little bundle as if it was the crown jewels. I turned Sara's head towards her daughter. "Sara," I said, "this is Olivia." I then repeated it by saying, "Sara, Olivia, Olivia, Sara," and pointing to each in turn as I spoke their name. Now if you ever meet me don't ask me why Sara did what she did next as I will be unable to tell you. Sara's eyes still staring out into space as they had done since day one now seemed to focus on little Olivia. Sara moved her hand towards Olivia and with her index finger half bent she placed it on Olivia's face. I could feel the tension from the nurses. Sara then carried out an act that will stay with me, and I am sure for all parties present, for ever: she placed her finger with the gentleness that only new mothers can show on Olivia's cheek and allowed it to caress and stroke the baby's cheek. "That's Olivia," I told Sara. She moved her eyes to meet mine and although there was no sound I'm sure I could hear her saying, "Yes I know, Dad, she's mine."

Sara then went back into that stupefying gaze that we had come to recognize over the last few weeks. I passed Olivia back to the person who stood next to me. I don't know who that was; I just walked away. I found myself in the family room thinking whatever divine person looks after children, thank you for my little girl. Over the next week or so the improvement in Sara's condition was outstanding. Even her consultant sat at the edge of her bed and could not believe what he was seeing. He explained to everyone at a later date that the recovery of patients in comas with blood clots can only be measured by the progress of each individual patient.

My Sara came out of her coma. She came home holding her little girl; she had made a full recovery. It seems that after tests ordered by St Mary's Hospital in Paddington, Sara had extremely high levels of the anti-cardio lipid syndrome with phospholipid antibodies and to stop her heparin injections at thirty four weeks had unfortunately caused her blood to clot over the following eight weeks until her stroke when Olivia was nine days old. The other girls who also had this particular syndrome had been fine after they had stopped the injections but because Sara's levels were so high she was the unlucky one. After what happened to Sara it was decided that all patients with this condition would be left on heparin until at least two months after they had given birth so that what happened to Sara should not and would not ever happen to anybody else.

The reaction to Sara's recovery from family and friends was amazing and just when we all thought it was safe to breathe again Sara announced that she and Paul had spoken to her specialist. They were saying that what had happened was and should be a 'one off' and if they wanted to have a second child there should be no reason for them not to try. Yes, you've guessed it! Paul and Sara were expecting their second child. I remember the day of Sara's first scan; I was at home when I saw their car pull up outside the house, Sara got out and ran to the door but I knew before she said anything, I knew that face. "I've lost it Dad. I'm so sorry," she said. After all this lass had been through she was still apologizing to me. Sara was told that her baby had died inside her but because of the treatment she was having to prevent her miscarrying it had done just that and stopped her actually losing the baby naturally so she had to wait a week until the hospital could perform a small operation and remove the baby.

Sara and Paul had already decided to try again as Olivia wanted a playmate and they were desperate for another baby so they tried one last time. That one last try resulted in a little brother for Olivia, born on the 17th January 2003 Elliot Baker Scott Corfield. Baker after her GP Dr Baker who had discovered her syndrome in the first place and Scott after her consultant who had looked after her during her pregnancy with both Olivia and Elliot. Sara and Paul later announced to everybody that their family was now complete. My last word on Sara's illness is that if any family deserves happiness it's Sara, Paul, Olivia and Elliot.

Sara, Elliot, Paul and Olivia

CHAPTER 25

It could be you

When I am called out to dogs in cars during a hot spell and if the owner returns as I am inspecting their beloved pet, panting its head off inside a vehicle with little to no proper ventilation, they always say the same thing, "I've only been gone a minute. The dogs alright, it's got plenty of fresh air." These lovely dog owners always seem to do the same thing when they get back into their car. Yes, you've guessed it; they start to wind down the windows. It gives me great pleasure in asking why they are doing it. The reply is not always printable but my cynical question always seems to hit the nail on the head. An inspector is authorised by our Society to take whatever action we feel is necessary to alleviate suffering and under the 1960 Abandonment of Animals Act, we don't have to prove that suffering has taken place, only that the act of leaving the dog in the car suffering was likely to take place. But an inspector has to document any evidence of likely suffering by finding out how long the dog was left, the outside temperature, the temperature inside the vehicle, the temperature of the dog, the state of the dog on arrival, how was it reacting, was it showing signs of distress, were there any witnesses to any of the above and did anyone take any action to alleviate the dog's distress prior to the inspector arriving? Not easy is it? Sometimes proving an animal did suffer by being left in a vehicle is easy but becomes very painful for the inspector to deal with.

One such case occurred on a hot day in the summer of 1997. A local businesswoman left her two boxer dogs in her vehicle whilst it was parked in the Crown Courts car park. The owner had stated that she had only intended being away for a few minutes but was in fact away for 3 hours on one of the hottest days of the summer. She had left what she thought was adequate ventilation and had left the vehicle at the time in shade. Her time in the court-house had taken longer than she had anticipated. I was asked to attend the car park after a security officer had broken into the vehicle to remove what he later described as two very distressed dogs. One of the dogs was in fact dead on removal from the vehicle. The second dog was rushed to a vet. It was in a coma and had to be put to sleep to alleviate its suffering.

A post mortem examination by the vet disclosed that the dogs had died through heat stress and suffered unnecessarily. I interviewed the dog's owner and like all people I have to speak to on these sorts of subjects she never thought it would happen to her dogs. Guilty was her plea and guilty was the magistrate's verdict, so please remember do not leave an animal in a vehicle for any length of time. It happened to this lady; next time it could be you!

CHAPTER 26

Special Constable

When I first applied to become a RSPCA inspector way back in 1970 I was at that time in the Nottinghamshire Special Constabulary but after successfully passing out from the RSPCA Headquarters in January 1971 I resigned my position in the Specials. The Society in those days did not encourage such activities, as it was almost impossible for an inspector to be off duty at any time to take up such activities. In 1983 I was visiting Ferndown Police Station, for what reason I can't remember, but I do know it wasn't to show a superintendent a piece of paper telling him of our new rules and regulations. I had just walked from one of the back rooms of the police station into the main office. I was having a conversation with one of the constables when I heard a voice coming from the front desk saying, "That voice sounds familiar, it sounds like John Norman." I turned and I saw a sergeant that I had not seen since the late 1960s when I was in the Specials in Mansfield. I recognized his smile and the pipe stuck in the side of his mouth. "Grenville," I replied. "Blimey, how long has it been?" I said to him as we shook hands and Grenville replied, "Too long." Grenville Richings was his name, Sergeant Grenville Richings, my long lost constable from Mansfield. We had a chat and it was from that reunion meeting that I applied to join the Dorset Special Constabulary. The RSPCA were more relaxed nowadays as inspectors had designated time off duty when neighbouring officers would cover his area.

Well it was thanks to Grenville that I remained in the Dorset Specials for just over 12 years. I rose to the dizzy heights of an inspector or as they called it in the Specials a sub-divisional officer. In fact I was the same rank in uniform in the Specials as the RSPCA. I was stationed in Ferndown but after promotion I went to Bournemouth Central. There I was the Senior Officer, responsible for the Specials not only at Bournemouth Central Police Station but also for Boscombe, Kinson and Winton police stations. I worked alongside the best regular officers you could ever wish to meet. It's understandable members of the public having a go at our police force when things don't go their way. Just remember that most serving officers would probably agree with the majority of the moans but they are governed by a higher body and they do, I can assure you, carry out their duties above and beyond what would normally be expected of them.

I was involved in some very funny and some very serious events during my time with the Specials. On one occasion I was awarded the Chief Constables Commendation. The citation read that I had shown courage and professionalism, initiative and prompt action therefore preventing serious injuries to others. I hope that I assisted the regular officers during my twelve and a half years and helped to make their difficult duties a little easier.

CHAPTER 27

Special Project Foster Parents

Yes that word 'special' plays a part in my life once again. When Sandra and I were in Pembrokeshire we decided to become foster parents and after the initial interviews with the social services and a general introduction to their rules and regulations we started taking in young children who were about the same age as Peter and Sara. Some of these kiddies just needed a short stay whilst one or both of their parents were away or possibly ill and in hospital, some we would have for a short stay from a children's home whilst preparations were being made for a permanent foster home for them. We found this short stay fostering very rewarding and just hoped that if anything happened to me and Sandra then maybe someone close would look after our kids the same way.

We continued this line of fostering on arrival in Dorset and for many years gave a home to numerous youngsters. After a few years the Dorset Social Services started to select experienced foster parents for a new system that was called 'Special Project Fostering'. Sandra and I agreed with their request for us to be included in this new venture. It was going to mean attending countless meetings, being educated on the laws concerning children in care, young juveniles, their rights, our rights, what could or could not be done, numerous courses to attend on drugs, mental abuse, physical abuse, sexual abuse, you name it and we attended a class on it. We worked alongside some very dedicated social workers and other foster parents became very good friends of ours over the years.

We fostered some very mixed-up juveniles. Some had been in and out of children's homes and foster homes for years and it was important that they settled down into adulthood. We had some good kids, some not so good and some, well let's leave it at that. I think you can understand why I will not go into this in any great detail. This chapter in my life is not to tell you about them it's just to enlighten you on what Sandra and I had been getting up to. However I will tell you about one lad. We met him when he was about 15. He had not had the greatest of starts in life and was reacting against this. It took two meetings before he would even stay in the same room as us. His name was Michael. He was a tall, handsome, fair-haired lad. One of the first lessons we had learned was that you had to wait until they decided to speak to you or co-operate with the social services and foster parents. If they rejected help there was very little anyone could do without causing all sorts of problems.

When Michael did finally decide to talk to us he came across as a complex character: arrogant, charming, violent, kind, rude and polite, but inside this make-up both Sandra and I saw a frightened boy who wanted to please but was untrusting of adults. After various meetings Michael agreed to try us out and he came to our home in Ferndown. He instantly hit it off with Peter and Sara. I am now going to skip the years that Michael was with us but what I will tell you is that young Michael left us, came out of the care of the social services and he turned his life around. When he left our home Michael could be proud of what he had achieved. He really was one of the success stories. But that's not the end of it, not by a long way. Although Sandra and I did not see him for several years Sara would tell us that she had seen Michael and that he seemed to be doing all right. He always asked Sara to remember him to us.

One day many years later I was at home when I answered a knock on the door. On my doorstep stood a tall, well-built young man and at his side was a small child. "Are you alright, John?" said the man. "Yes, fine. What do you want?" I replied. "You don't recognize me, John, do you?" he said. "No," I replied. At this point the young child tugged at my arm and I thought I heard him say, "Are you my granddad?" The words passed over me without me really taking them in. I looked up at the young man and asked, "How can I help you?" The young man smiled. He looked so familiar but I could not put a name to his face.

"It's me, John, Michael. I'm Michael," he said. A hundred pictures flashed through my mind and my filing system stopped on that frightened little boy all those years ago.

"Michael," I said as if I had recognized him from the moment I had opened the door, "where have you been"? He gave me a few answers and we ended up in the kitchen area of the house. The little lad kept tugging my sleeve as kids do. "Yes little man," I said to him bending down to his height, "and who are you?" I asked. "I'm Michael," he said, and as bold as brass, "are you my Granddad?" I looked up at big Michael with an obvious confused frown on my face. "John there's something I want to ask you and Sandra," he said. He then went onto explain that he was being asked all sorts of questions by little Michael, who was in fact now five years old, about where Daddy used to live when he was little and other difficult questions about grandmas and granddads. Now although Michael's partner Sharon had a mother living in the area that little Michael knew and called Grandma, there was an area in big Michael's life when he stayed with us that was becoming difficult to explain to little Michael.

"So," said Michael, "Sharon and I have told little Michael that he has a nana and granddad that looked after his daddy and one day he would take him to see them. Well John, Sharon and I were wondering if you and Sandra would be willing to let little Michael call you Nana and Granddad?" Well readers what would you say? How would you feel? Well when you've decided, that's exactly how I felt but ten times more. My heart was just about to burst when Sandra came home. I hushed Michael not to say who he was and I asked Sandra, "Do you know who this is?" "No I don't," she said as she ran an eye over the two Michaels. Not wanting to prolong her agony I came straight out with it. I told Sandra it was Michael and then I introduced little Michael and told her that there was also a daughter called Danielle who was only a few months old and that big Michael had got a partner called Sharon. I told Sandra about Michael's request regarding being called Nana and Granddad. Sandra hugged big Michael and picked up little Michael and

I am not ashamed to tell you all the adults had tears in their eyes as little Michael asked Sandra, "Are you my new Nana?" A few days later we met Sharon and lovely baby Danielle and from that day to this they have been a part of our family.

Sheryl and Peter

CHAPTER 28

The Finishing Post

Over the previous year I had given a lot of thought about my life and what direction I want it to go. On the 27th May 2005 I would be that grand age of 60 and after a long discussion with Sandra I decided that on Tuesday 16th August 2005 at 1700 hours I would take early retirement. If you haven't worked out the dates then I can confirm that it would mean I had been with the RSPCA for 35 years to the day. Where has it all gone? Well you have been down many of the roads with me and I am sure you will realise I have left many of them for another day. What is in the future for me? Well what I know is I've still got my little girl Sara, a great son-in-law in Paul, two grandchildren Olivia and Elliot that I would die for, not forgetting of course big Michael, little Michael who is now as big as his dad, Danielle who is now growing into a fine young lady, all being guided by the steady hand of Sharon.

Peter, that little lad who played come and get me with his mam all those years ago, is everything a parent would want. In December 2004 he invited Sandra and I to accompany him and his fiancée Sheryl, and what a lass she is, we love her to bits, to Australia. Peter and Sheryl were making plans to emigrate and we all went to look at the area in and around Perth. We flew over to Sydney and on 5th December 2004, on board a 40ft yacht, Peter and Sheryl were married with the Sydney Opera House and the Harbour Bridge as a backcloth. What a day!

Well my friends it's Tuesday, 16th August 2005 and it's 5p.m. I've made it; 35 years are behind me. They've come and they've gone. I thank each and every one of you for being with me on this journey. Last but by no means least; I thank Sandra for without Sandra being there, there would not have been the last 35 years.

My final wish is that for years to come I hope people will continue to say, **"Here comes Humanity Dick!"**

RSPCA

The Royal Society for the Prevention of Cruelty to Animals works tirelessly to promote kindness and prevent cruelty to animals.

The RSPCA is a charity and does not receive any government funding for its £82,000,000 annual running costs.

Donations, no matter how small, are always gratefully received.

For further information visit: -   www.rspca.org.uk

For any comments or further information on this book
Please contact the author: - jnorman@gotadsl.co.uk